About

HOW TO LOVE YOURSELF
WHEN YOU DON'T KNOW HOW

When you decide to lay the ghosts of your past to rest, Bishop and Grunte will be your best teachers. They combine the compassion of natural healers with the knowledge of skilled therapists. I recommend this book as a major step toward psychological self-healing.

Dr. Marlene Piturro
Author of *Business Finance* and *Late Bloomers*

Analyses of the psychological and spiritual healing processes are blended with a full measure of practical, take-home advice that is ready to apply to what hurts inside. It should help liberate those who have experienced childhood abuse, lack of confidence, low self-esteem, and shyness from the prisons of their own making.

Philip G. Zimbardo, Ph.D.
Author of *Shyness, What It Is, What To Do About It*

The authors have managed to distill the best of good therapies and have developed a practical, useable mode in which a lay person may operate. Surely this is one great leap on the road to good health.

Merna Popper
Founder & Publisher, *Women's News*

How to Love Yourself When You Don't Know How

Healing All Your Inner Children

Jacqui Bishop, m.s. & Mary Grunte, r.n.

Foreword by Philip Zimbardo, ph.d.

p•u•l•s•e

A P.U.L.S.E. Book, published by Station Hill Press, Inc., Barrytown, New York 12507.

Distributed in the United States by The Talman Company, 131 Spring Street, Suite 201E-N, New York City, New York 10012.

Cover and book design by Susan Quasha.

Library of Congress Cataloging-in-Publication Data

Bishop, Jacqui.
  How to love yourself when you don't know how : healing all your
inner children / Jacqui Bishop, Mary Grunte.
    p. cm.
  Includes bibliographical references and index.
  ISBN 0-88268-131-1
    1. Inner child. 2. Adulthood--Psychological aspects.
3. Psychotherapy. I. Grunte, Mary. II. Title.
BF698.35.I55B57 1992
158'.1--dc20   90-22712
                                                   CIP

Manufactured in the United States of America.

Contents

Foreword

Philip Zimbardo, Ph.D.

This is a book for all seasons, for all reasons. Its vital message should reach the teenager unsure of his or her direction in life and rebellious without knowing why. It is ideal for young adults who seem to have it all going for them, yet are more unhappy than satisfied. It's perfect for the older person whose life should be settled and stable, but is somehow empty of the contentment with which it should be filled. In reading this labor of love by Jacqui Bishop and Mary Grunte, each will discover the reasons for much of their discontent, the failure to connect fully with other people, and the missing ingredient that can fill every day with the miracle of life's wonders.

Most people feel some lack of satisfaction. Too many of us are unable to love those close to us as fully as we desire to and as much as they need us to, because we have not yet learned to love ourselves as we should. For others, career progress is uneven and uncertain, with advances and back-sliding alternating in troubling ways. And then there are our brothers and sisters who find their only solace in addictions to momentary pleasures that conceal deep suffering that must eventually surface.

Most solutions to these problems have a catch to them. Traditional psychotherapy can help some, but too many people fear taking their problems to a stranger-expert, don't know how or where to find one, and lack the financial resources to pay for a therapeutic relationship of sufficient duration. Being part of a social support network of caring friends and relatives alleviates part of the pain for others, but how many families and friends stick by an addict, hang in there to the end, for a person who is self-abusive and perhaps abusive of them as well?

An answer to many problems of dysfunctional patterns of behavior is presented by the authors in their conception of the Inner family, comprised of an Inner Grownup and Inner Children, who have not really completed their childhood apprenticeship but have commandeered the driver's seat, so to speak. To outward appearances, a person may seem to be an adult, play adult roles, be forced to accept the responsibilities and obligations of an adult. However, the person doesn't feel, and in fact is not, prepared to do so. When Inner Children occupy the driver's seat, a person is not yet ready for prime time enjoyment of the benefits of adulthood. For that, the Inner Children need to relinquish control to the Inner Grownup, the member of the Inner Family whose job it is to assume those adult responsibilities and to take care of the Inner Children as well.

Readers will find in this lovingly written book, the paths to love—love of self, love of others, and love of God as well. Analyses of the psychological and spiritual healing processes are blended with a full measure of practical, take-home advice that is ready to apply to what hurts inside. It should help liberate those who have experienced childhood abuse, lack of confidence, low self-esteem, and shyness from the prisons of their own making. In reading this book and actively engaging in the exercises it offers, you cannot help but reaffirm the power of the human connection, and be more receptive to the special dimensions of daily living that bless each of God's children.

Philip G. Zimbardo, Ph.D.
Professor of Psychology, Stanford University
Author of *Shyness, What It Is, What To Do About It,* and *The Shy Child*

Preface

"This is your racket, Jacqui. You're just ripping off strokes!" The rest of the group nodded wisely. I was stunned and speechless.

It was 18 months into my long struggle up out of the pit of suicidal depression. In the clinical jargon of transactional analysis, I had just heard my therapist accuse me of using all my work, all the time and money I was pouring into therapy, all the emotional agony I was in, simply as a "racket" or manipulation to get attention. My supposed "ally" had turned on me.

I left in a daze. "Could they be right?" I asked myself. My only response was despair, overwhelming and black.

"I could wring their necks! Just because they don't have the answers—don't you dare swallow that garbage!" If it hadn't been for Mary, indignant and protective on my behalf, I'm not sure how I would have handled it.

Privately, later, she wondered and worried over the possibility the therapist might be correct, but it never felt right; and if it didn't feel right Mary didn't buy it. Neither of us had answers any more than the therapist did, but we couldn't accept the idea that no answers existed and that, if they existed, we couldn't find them. In the meantime, Mary supplied the encouragement I needed to hang in; if I couldn't trust myself, I could trust her, and hope that her trust in me was justified.

I will always remember and be grateful to Mary's family for making space for me in their daily life, and especially to Leon, Mary's husband, for the open-hearted way he accepted our friendship. Not everyone did. Some accused us of being symbiotic—and they probably had a point: For a time, we did tend to finish one another's sentences (and had fun doing it), and we did trust and rely on one another's strengths—Mary, on my logical sequencing ability and communication skills, I on her incredible intuition. However, adult symbiosis tends to stifle growth, whereas in our case the reverse was true: each of us provided the other with instruction and modeling in a safe space of love and encouragement, and within that space we were able to reclaim and exercise the intuitive and intellectual gifts we'd relinquished as children. If that was symbiosis, it was the very best kind.

Technicalities aside, the bottom line was this: We were healing coaches to one another, committed to responding to the leadings of the Holy Spirit as best we knew how. It probably saved my life.

xii   HOW TO LOVE YOURSELF

I recovered, slowly, from the shock of the "racket" incident, and such was my dependence on the therapist that I chose to go back. I didn't know what to do instead, and I was too frightened to leap out into the unknown. Besides, caught in the dependency of a transferential relationship, I believed that, if this person couldn't help me, it might be that no one else had answers either.

And answers did begin to come, although mainly outside the therapy room.

The first breakthrough was my introduction to Jacquelina—an Inner Child who appeared to my mind's eye. She was huddled "in a corner," with her arms protecting her head, and she refused to budge or to return to my body. That may sound strange, but I could physically feel where she was supposed to be: It was as if I had a great egg-shaped cavity extending from my upper chest to my navel. Jacquelina was the first of the Inner Children we found who had decided that, no matter what the rest of me and my therapist wanted, she wasn't going to be part of it. She was holding out—for what? Depression? Crying all the time? What the hell did she want? She wouldn't dialogue with me, only with Mary. And she wouldn't shape up.

As time went on, I became more and more impatient: No way could I either fill this hole I felt in my body or create a visual picture in which Jacquelina came into line. I felt so angry, I used to scream in frustration. "That's a child," Mary would say. "No that's ME," I would snap. It came to a head one day as I was sitting in a boat out in the middle of a lake. I could feel depression begin to overcome me, and I was in a rage at Jacquelina, trying to blow out the heaviness with anger. This had worked in the past, as often as not, but this time I was getting nowhere. Finally, at an impasse, I cried out loud, "WHY won't you let go? Why do you insist on making me miserable? Why do you hate me?," and broke into sobbing.

What happened next permanently changed my internal relationships: Jacquelina began to talk to me, and what she said was this: "You treat me so badly; you don't care what I feel. All you want to do is be aggressive and angry and run all the time. Sometimes I just want to be quiet and rest or cry or get taken care of. Why are you so unkind to me?" All at once I saw that what she said was true. A long time ago, I had decided to protect her by acting outwardly as if I had no sadness. It didn't help to be sad, I had reasoned, so I wouldn't feel sad. To protect her, I'd be smart, and I'd keep on the move. But what I had done to protect Jacquelina had turned into a prison for her; she no longer had any outlet for her feelings, and I hadn't provided any internal source of comfort. In that moment, I remembered that I really cared about this Jacquelina, that she was my inner sister, and I felt overwhelmed by remorse over what I'd been doing. "I'm so sorry!" I cried. "Please, please forgive me. I promise I'll never do that again to you." She forgave me and in fact I never did do that again—not that way anyway.

This breakthrough wasn't the end, however, because I also saw that Mary was right: the part of myself that I considered ME was actually a child. Older by a couple of years than Jacquelina, her name was (and is) Jacklin. She's courageous, highly intelligent and, especially back then, ready to fight anyone or anything at the drop of a hat. So tight was her control that she pretty much filled my awareness most of the time, and, given her intellectual strength, learning to detect when my thinking was and wasn't adult took us a long time. I had a long way to go before my Grownup showed up (but the rest of that story belongs in another book).

Thus began the evolution of the Inner Family Healing technique described in the book you're now holding. For much of the way, I was mainly the guinea pig, and Mary was mainly the scientist. I say mainly, because we'd switch off. We'd also take other roles: reporter, detective, devil's advocate, cheerleader, observer. Sometimes someone else would step in as guinea pig, and then I would be therapist and Mary would be observer—or vice versa. And then, of course, we'd be all those roles for ourselves.

The gift of the "racket" incident was that it gave us a powerful impetus to find an easier, faster, less costly way to heal the mind and emotions: a way that would circumvent the need to form with a therapist a dependent, transferential relationship, a sort of symbiotic bond that must later be broken, often at great emotional cost to the client. Most of all, we sought a way that would affirm a person's own inherent power to heal—not without help, for we all need help, but with the greatest possible experience of personal autonomy right from the beginning of the process.

Much to our amazement, that is precisely what we did. The essence came clear in a very short time; what it boiled down to was this:

1. Within the normal human character resides a collection of personalities that resemble a family—an Inner Grownup and Inner Children of different ages.

2. Most of our difficulties in life arise from conflicts and imbalances in the power relationships, values, and demands that prevail among the members of this Inner Family. When one of the Inner Children is in the driver's seat, the person is probably headed for trouble.

3. Healing is the end product that results from reconciling these conflicts—that is, when our Grownup learns to assume control

of our whole person and unconditionally love, protect, and communicate with our Inner Children, and when each Inner Child trusts and accepts itself and bonds with the Grownup.

Working out the details, testing the process fully, and articulating it in this book took almost a decade. Today, the results are visible in our lives and in the lives of hundreds of clients, friends, and families.

We are thrilled at what Inner Family Healing is. First of all, it answers the question, "How do I love myself if I don't love myself already?" Most spiritual and self-help books today recommend you love yourself, but few tell you how. And if you don't know how to do it already, it's not so easy to learn. Inner Family Healing actually teaches you how to love yourself in specific, easy-to-understand steps, and, in our experience, it works for anyone who chooses to stick with it.

Second, Inner Family Healing is flexible, effective, efficient, and universal. It can be used alone or in conjunction with other techniques. It works faster and produces visible results more consistently than any other technique we know, either traditional or nonconventional. Despite its effectiveness, people with no special background have used it with no more difficulty—and sometimes less—than highly trained therapists. The most helpful background is exposure to a healthy family.

Although we hope the book will be read and used by therapists, counselors, people working with the sexually abused, and 12-step program participants, we've aimed it primarily toward people who wouldn't or couldn't enter therapy because of financial or other constraints. Thus it is for anyone who wants to love themselves, to discover and build self-esteem, to make their relationships more harmonious and nourishing, to claim their full power in work, and to enjoy life.

We suggest you reread the book at least once. These ideas may be unfamiliar, even strange, and some of the material may be quite disturbing. Just keep rereading until you develop confidence that you understand the theory. This will give you some sense of security with the whole thing so that, as you actually use the process, what happens will make sense faster and you'll have already absorbed some very important perspectives on taking good care of yourself.

Be kind to yourself as you read. There's no demand for perfection; there's no time limit; and you can learn as much from mistakes as successes. So whatever you do, simply observe what works and what doesn't. Our Inner Children are faithful teachers, no matter what you may think initially, and difficulties encountered today will turn into strengths tomorrow if you stick with it. Guaranteed.

We welcome feedback on the process. As much time and work as we've devoted to developing Inner Family Healing, we still learn something new practically every day, and we fully expect some of the readers of this book to take it far beyond what we could ever have imagined. We'd like to be in on the excitement, so please keep us posted!

In the meantime, we wish you courage, joy, love, and Shalom!

Jacqui Bishop
Mary Grunte
Box 97
Bronxville, N.Y. 10708
(914) 997-9611

This book is
lovingly dedicated to you, our reader

Acknowledgements

This book is a product of many minds and hearts beside our own. We now understand those authors who plead helplessly, "there are too many to name." Where we've borrowed discrete, readily distinguishable pieces of wisdom, we've given specific credit, but most sources of learning and encouragement have had such a subtle, indirect, or pervasive influence that to assign credit would be very difficult indeed. Having extended that apology to anyone who should have been acknowledged, we nevertheless press on to thank the following:

- ❖ Our families, who've supported us, taught us, endured us, and best of all, cheered us on. Thank you for your faith in us.
  - Leon Grunte, Irene Grunte, and John Grunte for giving up family time and space for the book.
  - Jeanne-Marie Bishop and Roger Bishop, for urging their daughter to reach for the highest good, and for their steadfast support, without which this book might not have been possible.
- ❖ Our clients, who taught us, corrected us, and shared their lives with us.
- ❖ The therapeutic pioneers on whose shoulders we stand: especially Eric Berne, Dan Casriel, the Gouldings, Steven Karpman, Jacqui Schiff, and Claude Steiner.
- ❖ Philip Zimbardo, who took time out of an enormously busy schedule to read our book, and, without reservation, to affirm our work. What a healing gift!
- ❖ Our teachers and therapists for the wonderful multi-disciplinary training that provided the foundation for the development of this thinking: Dan Casriel, Suzanne Dunn, Deborah Fay, Julie Firman, Marjorie Friedlander, Valerie Lankford, Francois Linane, Frankie Wiggins, and Steven Winners.
- ❖ George Kandle, to whom we owe special thanks: As Director of the TA/Gestalt wing of the Foundation for Religion and Mental Health, George was our principal trainer from 1977 to 1982. His superb mentoring and uncompromising demand for

excellence evoked in us an appreciation of and commitment to the highest standards of professional conduct in the healing profession.

❖ The Motley Crewmembers for loving and encouraging us and allowing us to practice on them over the years.

❖ Those friends who painstakingly labored through these pages, especially in the early and most disorganized stages: Jeanne Bishop, Roger Bishop, Jr., Eric Candrea, Wendell Carroll, Halya Duda, Demita Gerber, Leon Grunte, Lisa Haines, Lisa LaSalle, John Lawry, Myrna Tortorello, Bob Tyrka, Christie Van Kehrberg, and Elaine Zablotny.

❖ Others who contributed in a variety of ways, from writing vignettes to giving us printer time to photocopying: Diana Calder, Irene Grunte, Toni LaMotta, Ann and Gene Rathbun, Harold Snedeker, Judy Vaillancourt, Dennis Wilson, and Denise Young.

❖ Ken Binney, for his advocacy and encouragement, and for his insistence that we keep thinking bigger.

❖ George and Susan Quasha, publishers of Station Hill Press, who not only praised the book, but renamed and published it, in impeccable taste and in accordance with their commitment to make the world a better place in which to live.

Finally, we, each of us, want to thank each other, for more than we can say, but especially the following:

❖ I, Jacqui, thank Mary Grunte, without whose loving support I might never have discovered my intuitive gifts, Inner Children, or secrets of loving life.

❖ I, Mary, thank Jacqui Bishop, who so long ago helped me write a play and gave me the encouragement needed to develop the confidence that, indeed, I could be a writer.

1

INTRODUCTION

Reclaiming the Power to Love Ourselves

After years in the therapy room, we are firmly persuaded that all of us human beings are born into the world with a natural, inherent capacity for accepting and loving ourselves and others. However, for that capacity to develop as we grow, it must be nourished when we're small. That is to say, others, especially those directly responsible for our care, must appreciate and return our love both physically and emotionally. To the extent they fail to return this love, our ability to love ourselves and to give and receive love in relationships with others diminishes. And then we become poor for, truly, as Mother Theresa has said:

Poverty is not just being without food. It is the absence of love.

We believe this quote expresses an inner deprivation that most of us suffer to some degree. Our intention in writing this book is to respond to the poverty created by the absence of love for ourselves by showing how this next quotation can be fulfilled by you and within you:

Every child has been created for greater things—to love and be loved . . .

Inner Family Healing is a method for reclaiming the capacity for love and developing the skill to express that love. Using this method, people have improved the quality of their lives in work, in relationships, at play; enhanced problem-solving abilities; increased creativity and spontaneity; and accelerated the process of letting go of upsetting feelings.

Introducing the Inner Family

What do we mean by the Inner Family? "Inner" refers to what exists in a person's internal awareness, as opposed to what exists outside the body and can be seen by others. "Family" refers to patterns of thoughts, feelings, and behaviors that resemble a family structure of personalities and interactions.

You may not have thought of having an Inner Family in just those terms, but we can all identify words and phrases that run through our brains to tell us how we are or should be thinking, feeling, and acting in response to what's going on in our lives. When we listen carefully to these words and phrases, they begin to sound as if they are coming from particular personalities with distinctive characters. As we continue to observe, it becomes clear that some of these characters sound adult while others sound childlike. Moreover, their patterns of internal communication—both negative and positive—recall our own upbringing.

Let's take a closer look at the Inner Children and the Inner Grownup that comprise this Inner Family.

The Inner Children

Inner Children are the one or more young personalities we all have inside us. In many ways, these Inner Children are just like outer children— loving, curious, full of feeling and emotion, intelligent, and complete. They differ from outer children in that: (1) they share a physical body with an adult being—that is, you; (2) they are caught in a time warp: that is, even though the body they inhabit is fully grown, they still think they're physically small and proportionately vulnerable, especially to people who resemble their original caretakers in some way; (3) when threatened, they revert to behaviors that are related to unhappy events early in their lives, and they recreate the sense of helplessness, pain, rage, and fear that those original events evoked in them.

These Inner Children range in age from conception through the teens, and their mental, emotional, and behavioral patterns reflect those ages. For example, infant Inner Children mainly want to be cuddled, fed, stroked and allowed to sleep. They feel fear and love, but their anger responses are less well-developed than those of the two-year-olds, for example, who are experimenting with the concept of NO. Ten-year-olds are reaching for experiences of mastery on a new level. Teenage Inner Children are concerned with what their peers think, are preoccupied with the challenges of learning social skills, are struggling to accommodate enormous sexual changes, and are working to establish themselves as separate from their parents.

If you're bothered by the idea that you have Inner Children running around inside you, you're not alone. At one point or another, we've been bothered, too, as have most of our clients. We urge you to reserve judgment for a while and read on. If you have Inner Children, you're not a victim of multiple personality disorder, or if you are, so is everybody else. Over 95 percent of the people we've worked with (in settings ranging from corporations to parking lots) identify their Inner Children, connect with them, and begin developing a positive relationship with them in under an hour or two. And it's not surprising—these Inner Children are made up of our own memories and our own emotional, thinking, and behavioral patterns at various ages, and so they are part of what makes every one of us who we are.

So having Inner Children is as natural as having two ears and a nose, and Inner Children aren't abnormal or alien, nor does their presence in any way prevent us from being whole, integrated, and in charge of ourselves. Quite the contrary: The quality of our lives expands and deepens as we get to know and learn to care for them properly.

Regardless of our chronological age, we can all identify times when we have acted more like children than adults. Those are the times when our Inner Children have temporarily taken over the personality because their needs have not been properly met by the Inner Grownup.

The Inner Grownup

The Grownup is the part of us that, as soon as we are biologically grown (around 18 or 20, let's say), has responsibility for carrying out the functions of a legal adult—holding a job, driving a car, caring for a family, and, most of all, taking care of ourselves.

When a person's Inner Grownup fully loves and properly cares for every one of the Inner Children, the person experiences a sense of wholeness, health, and joy, as well as love for self and others, regardless of what outer circumstances and related feelings may also be present. The internal power structure is balanced, which means the Inner Grownup takes into account feedback from self, Inner Children, and trusted others in the situation and makes the best decision it can for the benefit of the whole Inner Family.

To get a sense of your own Grownup functioning, recall the last time that you felt in control of a situation, full of energy, and open, unafraid, caring, and clear about what needed to happen for you and for others. You may have been aware of a physical sensation of balance and connectedness with the earth. You may have seen with fresh compassion the funny side of life. That's an experience of a fully functioning, powerful Inner Grownup.

Not all of us can recall such an experience of Grownup functioning. That doesn't mean we don't have a Grownup—everyone has one somewhere unless they're brain-damaged—but it does mean that the Grownup is underdeveloped and has failed to assume responsibility.

What Happens When the Inner Grownup Fails to Take Responsibility for the Inner Children

We all missed out on some kind of parenting. In the ideal world, our biological parents would have modeled all the essential parenting skills, and our Grownup would have absorbed those parenting skills by osmosis. However, because no parent is perfect in all areas, and parents can't teach what they themselves don't know, every Inner Grownup lacks information and appropriate role models in some areas. Many are poorly equipped for the job of taking care of their Inner Children.

When our Grownup is ill-equipped, we tend to resort to behaviors that are ill-suited to adult life because in some respect, they disregard the connection between action and consequences. Such behaviors include, for example, misusing authority, evading responsibility, manipulating, rebelling, or behaving in other ways we used to when we were physically too small to defend ourselves or care for our own needs in an adult world.

For example, some people grow up in families where the rule is, Never Show Anger. They don't know that expressing irritation to communicate a need or want at the time it comes up is healthy and normal behavior and important to a person's well-being. Such persons may have trouble with depression (anger turned inward), difficulty protecting themselves from others' thoughtless or unscrupulous behavior, or trouble with explosions of temper over inconsequentials because of the backlog of anger. Further, they may choose to team up with someone who embodies all the anger that they themselves do not express. Inability to express anger can produce any one of a number of behavioral patterns, of which the following is just one example.

George was an attractive, well-organized, and respected man who held a responsible position as a department head in a large insurance agency. But as well as he did his work, he would be passed over for promotion, again and again. It was for this reason that he came into therapy.

In the sessions, we learned that whenever a male peer or superior raised his voice in anger, George would rush to fix whatever the person was upset about, whether or not he was responsible for doing so. He reported that when he behaved this way, he would feel young and frightened. As he learned about how the Inner Family was supposed to work, he realized that his Grownup was allowing 3-year-old Little George to assume control.

George also saw he was acting the way he used to 30 years ago when his father was angry. When George was little, his father would walk around silent, but clearly furious. George, terrified he would be the target, would say, "I'm sorry," and rush to make his father happy—and it worked most of the time, at least often enough to persuade Little George that appeasement was the best coping tactic. And it probably was, at the time, for a child. For an adult working man, however, it was not.

Despite his abilities, George's progress in the company was stopped because his inability to handle anger directed at him was viewed as a severe flaw in his managerial capabilities. People had him pegged as a pushover, someone who could be manipulated by a simple show of irritation.

There's a happy ending, which is that George reeducated his Grownup using the Inner Family healing process. Much to the consternation of his co-workers, Pushover George shifted gears. Today it is George's Grownup, not Little George who handles angry men. Because of the difficulty of overriding the prevailing opinion of him at his job, George took another position at a competing firm, where his abilities are fully appreciated, and he is receiving acknowledgment for his talents, both verbally and concretely, in promotions and salary increases.

Even if an Inner Grownup doesn't know how to do its job properly, it continues to be responsible for all the Inner Children anyway. The Grownup may cry, "It's not fair, I'm not ready." However, the buck stops here: From the time we become legal adults, no one else has—or can take—responsibility for us. Ignorant or not, we're stuck with being responsible for our Inner Children.

Consequently, we are like most biological parents when it comes to parenting our Inner Children—untrained drivers in the driver's seat. Time and the car keep moving whether we want them to or not.

Sometimes the one in the driver's seat isn't the Grownup at all, but one of the Inner Children. In such cases, no matter how old we are chronologically, we behave like children, because the Inner Grownup has abdicated, has turned power over to an Inner Child. Havoc can ensue. Here's an example.

> Near where we live is a one-lane tunnel that serves two-way traffic. Only about 30 feet long, the tunnel is small in every dimension. Stop signs stand on either side of the tunnel. When cars are lined up in both directions, the common practice is for cars on either side of the tunnel to take turns going through, one at a time.
>
> From time to time, two drivers on opposite sides of the tunnel decide to pass through the tunnel at the same moment. They're going too slowly to crash; they just meet and glare. Every couple of months, the impasse becomes so prolonged that the police must be called to break up the deadlock. They arrive to find in the darkness of the little tunnel, two drivers glaring at one another across their steering wheels, each waiting for the other to back up and neither one willing to give an inch.

Inner Family Healing and How It Works

"Healing" means to restore to a healthy condition, to make sound, to reconcile. Inner Family Healing, then, means reconciling to one another the various Inner Children and the Grownup that constitute the Inner Family in each of us and restore a proper balance of roles in which the Grownup assumes responsibility for the Inner Children. As in outer families, the key is educating the Grownup to:

1. Maintain positive emotional contact with each of the Inner Children
2. Communicate with these Inner Children to discern their needs
3. Meet the Inner Children's needs in appropriate ways.

When the Grownup performs all these tasks, a person becomes capable of empowered living—that is, living in the present—because one has forgiven others, the past, and all the Inner Children. Only then do we take full responsibility for ourselves and our actions.

To extend the metaphor of car and driver: Inner Family Healing is like a concentrated driver training course. It doesn't guarantee a life free from tickets, accidents, bad weather, fears, and breakdowns, but it does give you an instruction booklet, and people to help you do things like parallel park your car until you've learned to operate and maintain it yourself.

HOW TO GET THE MOST OUT OF THIS BOOK

To get the most out of this book, we suggest you follow three recommendations:

1. Read the book through to the end so you understand each part in the context of the whole process.
2. Choose a healing coach.
3. Consider asking assistance from God, or your Higher Power, however you define that Power.

Read the Whole Book Through Before Beginning the Process

We recommend you read the entire book at least once before beginning to use the methods it describes, so you'll have a good feel for the overall process and for the relative importance of different parts of it. That way, if any difficult memories arise, you'll be better equipped to deal with the Inner Children who bring them up. We put the instructions for the first and second sessions in chapters 4 and 5 because you need that information to understand some of the rest of the book, but merely skim them until you're ready to actually do the process.

As you read, mark any passages that are upsetting to you, along with any thoughts you're aware of, and return to them when you begin to do the process. Such feelings are cues that something similar to what you've read may have happened to the Inner Children. They are also cues that the Inner Children are alive and well and need your Grownup's attention.

The book includes everything you'll need to get started: (1) a basic description of how the method works; (2) examples showing how to express unconditional love toward your Inner Children; (3) personal accounts describing particular Inner Families and their dynamics so you can get a sense of how others have experienced this process; and, finally, (4) a reference section suggesting books and sources of additional support for learning to love yourself.

Choose a Healing Coach

If you know and can afford to go into therapy with a therapist who understands or is willing to experiment with this process personally and then help guide you through it, by all means do so (especially if the chapters on abuse apply). We all need human encouragement and assistance, whether or not we want to admit it. Learning to love yourself when you haven't been able to usually requires at least a cheerleader, preferably a coach, and, better still, someone whose own life is a model for learning new and better ways of treating yourself.

If you don't have access to a therapist, consider choosing a friend to accompany you on this inner journey. In selecting such a friend—or a therapist, for that matter—look for one whose strengths complement your weaknesses. You need, between the two of you, to be able to come up with certain talents and skills. That means at least one of you must:

1. Genuinely like and enjoy you
2. Feel comfortable with children of various ages
   a. Enjoy children
   b. Naturally attract children
   c. Play like a child
3. Take charge as an adult when appropriate
   a. Take good care of personal needs without diminishing the well-being of others
   b. Be caring toward others in a way that encourages and empowers them rather than making them dependent
   c. Be comfortable coaching others.

If you don't find all the attributes you seek in one person, you may need more than one healing coach. If you don't know anyone who looks appropriate, don't despair. Ask around and join a group for a short time until you find someone—or that someone finds you! The key characteristic to look for is an atmosphere of encouragement. By the way, close relatives, romantic partners, and spouses can be helpful at first, but they generally share ignorance with you—that is, they need to learn the same lessons, so they don't usually make the best coaches for the long term.

Consider Asking God or Your Higher Power to Assist You

This section is for those who want to include a Higher Power in their Inner Family Healing process.

Although we are both Christians, and we believe that the Inner Family Healing method is a gift from God, you needn't be a Christian or spiritually inclined in any way for this process to work. It works anyway.

We do think, however, that the process becomes considerably easier when you consciously include Christ, God, or your Higher Power. We are such finite beings, and parenting—even just parenting ourselves—can sometimes seem a superhuman task. In moments of honesty, almost all parents will tell you they wish they had more Divine assistance so they could be sure of having the strength, wisdom, and love their children need. We sometimes think of God as the Grownup's Grownup—a source of power when we've run out of our own.

If you are open to working with God as part of your Grownup's cram course, we suggest you ask Him to help you now. Either silently or aloud, using our words or your own, pray for help in:

1. Learning to call on Him
2. Strengthening your Grownup with the love and compassion you need to nurture, guide, and protect your Inner Children
3. Healing the memories and decisions that keep your Inner Children imprisoned and alienated from each other, from other people, and from God.

❖

In the next chapter, we offer an overview of the Inner Family Healing process that will serve as a framework for understanding the rest of the book.

2

OVERVIEW OF THE HEALING PROCESS

Breaking the Family Spell

The power of Inner Family Healing becomes more vivid and easier to comprehend when seen against the backdrop of what we've labeled the Family Spell. To a greater or lesser extent, all of us superimpose the experience of past relationships over present ones. We then activate the emotional reactions, assumptions, and behaviors that we believe helped us survive those early relationships. This phenomenon, which is what keeps us in psychological bondage, is what we refer to as the Family Spell.

People don't usually begin breaking out of the Family Spell until they becomes so uncomfortable with their lives that they are willing to change anything to get relief. However, we *can* make the same changes *before* life becomes so painful. In either case, the following gives us what we need to break free:

1. An understanding of the Family Spell and what keeps it in place
2. A vision of what life could be like without the Spell
3. A systematic way to implement that new vision.

The Family Spell and How It Works

The Family Spell is a mental/emotional construction that replicates the structure and dynamics of power and love relationships as they evolved in our own families. We call it a spell because we operate within its confines as if we were bewitched into thinking that the way life was in our past is also the way life has to be now. We act as if we've been brainwashed or hypnotized into believing that no options exist other than those available in relationships that we had as children. In fact, we don't even question whether things can be different from what they used to be for us when we were small.

What It's Like To Be Under the Spell

As people learn about the Family Spell, they describe being caught in it in a variety of ways. All these descriptions contain one common element: the speakers feel as if they were operating in an altered state, in which their ability to see, hear, or act is somehow impaired. Here are some typical examples:

> DONALD. Operating under my Family Spell is like having blinders on, where I can only see what's right in front of my nose. I act and sometimes feel like I'm in a trance. Only later, when I look back at something I did under the Spell, do I see the broader spectrum of options that were available to me.

> JANE. I'm actually caught in my Family Spell right now in one area of my life. I'm frightened to complain to my upstairs neighbors. This man has been there a year now, crashing around like he wanted to go through the floor. I'm scared if I say something he'll just get worse and get disagreeable as well. I know in my head he's just a human being, but every time he shows up I just want to run—or kill.

> Sometimes I think my head has a filmstrip of all my past relationships running around it. As long as the filmstrip keeps spinning, it's almost invisible and I can see beyond it fairly well. However, when I meet someone who's like a person in my history, the filmstrip stops with the picture of the person in my past lined up in front of my eyes between myself and them. Whoever the person in my filmstrip is, the picture interferes so much that I can't connect with real here-and-now situations.

> One of these days I'll get myself to turn off the filmstrip projector and wake up to a wider reality. I'll go up to those people upstairs and let them know they need to lighten up or they'll get bone spurs

on their heels. It'll probably all work out and then I'll say, 'What was wrong with me? How could I have been so silly?'

Jane's metaphor of the revolving filmstrip provides us with a picture to help us understand how our past interferes with our present. Here's the picture: The filmstrip encircles our head, whirling constantly. As long as it keeps whirling, we can see pretty well beyond it to the people in the here and now. However, whenever someone we meet resembles a character on our filmstrip, the filmstrip stops, interposing that character's image in front of our eyes so that we can barely see the real person.

Because of this, we can see others clearly only to the extent that they do not resemble or act like anyone from our past who frightened us. To the extent they do resemble someone in our past, our perceptions will be distorted, for good or ill.

Let's take a look at how the Family Spell might appear in the filmstrip of George, the ex-pushover we met in chapter 1. Here are just a few of the pictures that George's filmstrip would contain: (1) The picture of him with his gentle, doting grandfather shows George as a sweet and compliant child, available to be nurtured without fear of judgment. (2) In relationship to his violent and abusive alcoholic father, he is in a power struggle of fluctuating intensity, with corresponding shifts in his image—from profoundly angry to deviously rebellious to helpless, needy, and frightened. (3) In the picture of him with his overprotective, ambitious, and driving mother, he is a sulky, stubborn 4-year old, immovable and secretly enraged in the face of her endless demands and domination. (4) In the picture of George with his younger brother, he is a nasty bully, finally able to assume a position of power instead of weakness, rejecting and persecuting his brother at every chance.

The more threatened we felt in the early relationship, the more distorted our reactions tend to be in here-and-now situations that recall those early relationships. So, for example, George reacts in a more extreme way to people who act or look like his abusive father than he does with people who act like his grandfather. When a man shouts in anger, George reacts either in terror and helplessness, or in devious rebellion, and always he's ready to flee. He's less extreme with a woman; he may push her away, but he doesn't manifest the same evidence of underlying terror. By contrast, when George meets someone whose emotional profile corresponds to that of his gentle grandfather, he feels safe and happy, and he expects and usually gets nurturing attention. And when he meets anyone who seems needy and vulnerable, like his younger brother, he becomes a sneaky bully, sending out nonverbal signals of rejection and hostility, and thinking and speaking in ways that denigrate the other person, the way his father denigrated him. Every one of us could point to similar examples in ourselves or others.

While under the Family Spell, although we have access only to the positions depicted on our filmstrip, we can switch positions in the power struggle if the situation permits. In other words, though we may have been the helpless one facing a bully, we can choose to be the bully instead. This is what often produces the pecking-order syndrome that occurs between siblings. What is dished out to kid number one, number one kid usually passes down in like manner to number two, as George did, or to the next kid of the same gender.

Fortunately, and most important, we also have the power to assume positions beyond the Family Spell, to take actions the Family Spell does not include. Although our filmstrip never totally disappears and we will always have some tendency to see the present through the veil of the past, the Family Spell *can* be broken. We can acknowledge the filmstrip as a memory that had validity for the past, but that no longer need run us. George no longer needs his grandfather to nurture him. He is now a full-grown adult, adequately equipped to nurture his own Inner Children.

What enables us to exercise this power to move beyond the Family Spell is the process of injecting the realities of the present into our memories of the past. As long as we operate according to the filmstrip, our surroundings will tend to respond to our actions in ways that reinforce our original decisions. But by intervening in old scenes, our Grownup interrupts that loop of actions and reactions.

As any good student of fairy tales can tell you, however, spell-breaking is serious, sometimes tricky business, and we are grateful that a proverbial good fairy shows up when one is ready to help oneself.

What Keeps the Spell in Place— Pseudo-free Choices

As children, we make choices in reaction to what happens to us. These choices aren't bad; in fact, they may have been appropriate at the time. But they're based on the past, when we were truly at someone else's mercy instead of on the present, when we have all the power and freedom of being an adult. Thus, although they may look like free choices, they are not. These pseudo-free choices fit one of three basic models:

1. I reject power and I will always be a victim. I lose.
2. I'll be the powerful one. I win.

3. I won't play the game at all.

None of these three types of decisions breaks the Family Spell. On the contrary, every one of them serves to keep the Spell in place, *because they offer no options apart from what is available on the filmstrip:*

1. *I reject power and I will always be a victim.* George is an example of someone who chose this position. Here are some of the thoughts and feelings that keep this choice of the victim role in place: (1) Power is bad—I know because I was in someone's power who hurt me over and over. (2) If I try to be powerful, I'll get hurt even more than I did back then. (3) I never want to be like the awful person who hurt me. (4) If I take enough punishment, maybe I can keep it from ever getting worse.

   Although we may avoid perpetuating the original abuse pattern as abusers and we may even feel righteous about being better people for it, we're quite likely to continue suffering abuse ourselves because we've given away the only access to power that we know. *And because we continue to subject ourselves to others' abuse when we no longer have to do so, we must assume responsibility with the abuser for the harm the abuser does us.*

2. *I'll be so powerful no one will ever treat me like that again.* This choice involves switching positions: Instead of assuming the helpless or weak position we occupied as a child, we move to the position occupied by the powerful character we're relating to. This type of choice alters somewhat the way we experience the Spell: We have access to some power, we can use it to control the situation in our own defense, and we have outward targets on which to vent our old anger.

   People who choose this position of overt control fall into one of two categories: Hero or Villain. Each of these positions has its advantages and disadvantages: On the upside, being a Hero looks better to society and gives us some pride in being "good." Being a Villain enables us to be open about our anger instead of expressing it covertly through control. Both positions allow us to claim and use our personal power and avoid domination by others.

   On the downside, however, both positions have serious drawbacks. Choosing to be the person in control produces harmful results to self and others because it restricts other people's freedom and puts them down. And, internally, we suffer much the same experience whether we choose to be heroic or villainous in that we spend enormous amounts of energy resisting any signs of what we would consider weakness in ourselves. If we are feeling weepy or frightened, we often turn on ourselves in outrage at what we perceive as our cowardice, laziness, stupidity, or lack of attention. This turning on ourselves is actually the attack by an older Inner Child against a younger, victimized Inner Child.

Thus, although choosing to be powerful or "good" looks like a new choice, it can actually leave us just as trapped in the past as we were before, in that we're still reacting on automatic to the original experience of having been abused.

3. *Power is bad so I won't be powerful, but I don't want to get hurt, so I won't play.* Even the third choice, refusing to occupy any of the positions depicted on the filmstrip, leaves us trapped in the Spell, for we are still operating in reaction to the past. We see war consuming the rest of the world because it's on our filmstrip. We can't see peace even if we're in the middle of it!

Actually, very few of us really succeed at "not playing." Successful hermits are very rare. Isolation is costly for a species as social as homo sapiens. What tends to happen is a person creates a series of carefully controlled routines—work, shopping, meetings with casual acquaintances in predictable activities—and gradually, through lack of stimulation, becomes more and more depressed. Life loses color and taste. The sense that "no one understands me" grows because the person gives no one a chance to understand or misunderstand. To deal with the rising backlog of unmet needs, the person must become ever more negative or frozen toward the outside world.

Because we fail to understand why none of our so-called choices breaks the Family Spell, many of us go through life spinning from one position to the next and round again: getting hurt, hurting others in revenge, and retreating in hurt, fear, and rage. Eventually, hunger for human contact drives us back out into the world and we run into people just like so-and-so who was so mean. This either drives us back to our cave or to battle with the person, vainly trying to change them. It never works, so, eventually, we withdraw again until our hunger for human contact drives us back to repeat the cycle.

Fighting against the Family Spell using any of the three decisions we've described only strengthens it. The most painful part of being trapped in the Spell, regardless of what position we choose, is that *we continue to inflict on our Inner Children, our very selves, the same patterns we swore as children we would never allow or repeat* when we grew up. For example:

- We take care of the needs of others at the expense of our own.
- We entrust our Inner Children to the care of others who then violate our boundaries physically, mentally, emotionally, or spiritually.
- We overindulge the Inner Children, allowing them to do something in the short-term that sabotages their—and our—longer term well-being (e.g., buy something we can't afford, eat or drink something that will sicken us, do something for fun on impulse that will leave us in a bind later, try compulsively to finish work that can never be finished).

    Those overindulgences may either echo or contradict the way we were raised.

Regardless of which position we assume, we are repeating and thus reinforcing old patterns of rescuing, abuse, suffering, and withdrawal. Fighting directly against old patterns simply strengthens them.

To interrupt this, to move us out of the Family Spell altogether, another, more creative strategy is called for.

Key to Breaking the Spell: A New Vision

The challenge to the Grownup is to focus attention and energy on establishing new patterns based on an entirely new vision.

Much of the reason many of us act the way we do is that we literally don't know any better. What fills our vision is the filmstrip of the environment and characters with whom we grew up—and they didn't know any better either. They couldn't teach us what they didn't know.

To learn loving behavior toward our Inner Children, we need to replace the filmstrip with a clear vision of the kind of relationships we want to have, and then we need to make a commitment to bring that vision into reality. The Inner Family Healing process provides us with both: a new vision and the means for establishing that new vision in our lives.

Developing a clear vision of what we want to become as the first step along the way to getting or becoming what we want isn't a new idea, of course. Sages and creative people have been touting the power of setting clear objectives for millennia.

Why is having a vision so important? We can do little to improve on the answer provided by Robert Fritz in his book, *The Path of Least Resistance*, which explains with remarkable clarity a concept that Fritz calls "structural tension." Structural tension is what enables us to live creatively, to define and commit to a goal for ourselves and then make that goal a reality in our lives. This involves three steps: (1) having an inner mental and emotional "vision" of what you want for yourself; (2) seeing where you are at the moment; and (3) seeing clearly the contrast between the current and desired realities. The discrepancy between our vision and our current reality creates the structural tension, which is what pulls events from the current reality toward the desired or "created" reality.

Forming the Vision

We recommend you formulate your own vision of what you want for yourself using two main images, one internal and one external:

1. The healthy Inner Family
2. Models: people you know who already love and care for themselves, who *do* meet their Inner Children's needs.

The Healthy Inner Family

Your vision and appreciation of the healthy Inner Family will evolve, clarify, and deepen as you achieve it. You'll have a firm foundation for that process if you begin by studying these major characteristics of the healthy Inner Family:

1. *The Grownup is the "Executive."* A healthy Inner Family is one in which the Executive, the Inner Family member in charge, is the Grownup, not one or more of the Inner Children. This means that the Grownup: (a) takes full responsibility for what the person does; (b) stays aware and open to all parts of the personality and responds appropriately to them; and (c) operates in a way that takes into account the long-term well-being of the whole person.

2. *The Inner Children's needs are taken care of abundantly.* "Needs" covers protection, love, and nourishment—physical, mental,

emotional, and spiritual. When realizing it has failed to meet a need, the Grownup apologizes to the Inner Child, asks forgiveness, and then takes care of the need.

3. *No part of the Inner Family makes any other part wrong.* The Inner Family works in harmony. The Inner Children trust and approve of the Grownup and vice versa. All members of the Inner Family accept other members' feelings and thoughts as valid and honor them, although not necessarily as requested. No Inner Family member feels the need to close off or deny any other part of the Family—quite the contrary.

We can't actually see an Inner Family—it's an internal construct—but people with a healthy Inner Family love themselves. So for the more tangible part of your vision, we recommend you seek out as models people whose treatment of themselves bespeaks acceptance, respect, and affection.

People Who Already Love Themselves

People who love themselves are easy to spot. Their gaze is direct, they tend to have a compassionate sense of humor toward themselves and others, they enjoy children, and they are surrounded by an atmosphere of peacefulness. They can express feelings, make mistakes, and laugh, all without a sense of self-consciousness, shame, or righteousness. They have ample energy and they tend to express creativity, for its own sake, in small and large ways.

In getting to know such people, we discover that they do certain things to maintain and reinforce what works in their lives. Here's what they do and what you can look forward to more of in your own life; the ability to:

1. *Tune into themselves* for
   a. Signals of physical need or want (for food, rest, solitude, touch, sex)
   b. Signs of emotional deprivation (feeling sad, lonely, angry, frightened, overloaded)
2. *Respond to their physical and emotional needs* by exploring the form and timing in which the need or want can best be met, and then taking action to meet the needs
3. *Encourage themselves in creative behavior*, no matter how small or inept the beginnings

4. *Actively cultivate joy* in their daily experience of simply existing
   a. Remind themselves that joy and peace are available to all
   b. Train themselves to focus on the joyful aspects of living
5. *Take responsibility for what happens to them and for the way they feel about it* and communicate that to others where appropriate
   a. If they catch themselves getting into the blaming game of assigning cause for misfortune outside themselves, they stop, choose to forgive the circumstances, God, and any others, and explore how they caused what happened.
   b. If they feel sad or angry about something, they'll say something like, "I caused or allowed this. Have I asked for what I want? What will I do in the future to make sure I don't feel this way?"
6. *Accept and forgive themselves* when they fall short of their own or others' standards. For example, when they find themselves acting unloving or careless or irritable, they recognize it, forgive themselves, and go on to get what they need.

If you are just embarking on the Inner Family Healing process, you might want to take a moment right now to reread and think about these two images—the healthy Inner Family and people who love themselves—and create your own vision. What would your own family have looked like had it been healthy? Who would you pick as a model of someone who loves themselves?

When you think of how your life will be different if you bring this vision into reality, what do you feel? Do you feel happy? Or do you feel nervous and edgy, or angry, or sad? If your responses to the vision feel upsetting to you, then you need to deal with the underlying obstacles.

Handling Your Resistance to Getting What You Want

The biggest obstacles, Fritz says, to realizing our desired vision, what he calls our "created reality," are: (1) we don't actually want what we say we want, or (2) we have some fears about what will happen if we get it. Fritz recommends testing the power of our desire for the created reality we define by asking this question:

If someone presented our created reality to us on a plate, no strings, would we take it?

If we experience our answer as an unequivocal YES! with our mind, heart, and body congruent, then we know that our intention is clear. If not, then we must:

1. Reexamine our created reality to see what's in the way
2. Incorporate our ambivalent feelings and thoughts into the definition of current reality
3. Renew our awareness of the discrepancies between them to reinforce the structural tension.

Here's an example:

I say I want a clean attic, but week after week, I don't clean it up. I ask myself, If someone did it for me, would I accept the clean attic? I feel fear and a sense of loss. I realize that my ballet things are all up there and that I've been holding onto them as a way of holding onto the dream I had of being a ballerina. I don't want to let go of that dream. So I redefine my present vision of the cluttered attic, including all my ballet clothes and all my feelings about not wanting to let that dream go. I look at the enormous difference between what's there and what I want, and I reaffirm my vision of a clean attic. Pretty soon, an idea comes for how to deal with my ballet dreams, and I take my ballet equipment down to my young niece, who cherishes similar dreams. Perhaps she will make them come true. And then, slowly, the attic begins to look more and more like what I envisioned.

Once you've confirmed that your desire for your new vision is clear, you have something with which to begin replacing the Family Spell. You're now ready to launch into the first stage of healing the Inner Family. Don't worry if you feel your new vision of the Inner Family still seems sketchy or weak: You'll be clarifying and strengthening the vision with every step you take through the three stages of Inner Family Healing.

The Three Stages of Inner Family Healing

Although each person progresses through the Inner Family Healing process in their own unique way and at their own pace, everyone eventually completes three basic stages.

1. *Contacting the Inner Children and establishing an emotional bridge between them and the Grownup.* The Children tend to have specific physical locations in the body, and in this first stage, we begin by identifying the location and helping the person to make physical contact and begin speaking with and listening to the first Inner Child.

2. *Committing to the new vision in Inner Family terms.* The power of the new vision we talked about in the previous section is accessed when our Grownup commits to assuming full responsibility for the Inner Children.

    Often the Inner Grownup has abdicated this responsibility up to now, and the prospect of caring for its Inner Children feels overwhelming. There are many reasons for this sense of overwhelm: Perhaps the Grownup fears failure. Or perhaps making a commitment without having any idea of how to carry it out feels irresponsible or dishonest. Perhaps the Grownup lacks the skills. Perhaps the Grownup has taken on the feelings felt by the person's original biological parents.

    Regardless of the cause, the person must realize that what is happening now is *already* failure. Success can only begin with choosing to do the very best one can, so that if it's humanly possible to assume responsibility for the Inner Children, that's what the person will do.

3. *Teaching the Grownup how to respond to the Inner Children's needs.* Because our imperfect parents were the ones who taught us how we should be taken care of, we tend to fail our Inner Children in the same way our parents failed us at the same age. Three *basic principles of parenting* provide a framework for rectifying those early parenting errors.

    a. *The Grownup is **always** responsible for behavior.*
        Regardless of how imperfect, inadequate, tired, angry, fearful, and ignorant the Grownup may feel, there is no time off. There are no vacations for the Grownup. However, some Grownups aren't yet aware of this. For example, many of us attend a party with only an Inner Child present. We may stay up too late, drink too much, make a pass at the wrong person, or otherwise create dilemmas that will trouble us the next day. This is not the failure of the Inner Child; it's the failure of the Grownup to set and enforce appropriate

limits (when to go home, when to stop drinking, who is and isn't an appropriate person to hug and kiss, and so on).

When the Grownup fails the Inner Child, there are no excuses. The only thing the Grownup can do is ask forgiveness for letting the Inner Child down and commit to doing better next time.

b.   *Inner Children's thoughts and feelings are **always** OK.*

When our Inner Children feel angry or think violent thoughts, they need permission to feel and express those feelings and thoughts in a safe way. Once expressed and acknowledged as coming from the Inner Child and not the Grownup, the feelings begin to disappear.

In and of themselves, neither feelings nor thoughts have power to affect others. Actions are what affect others, and the Grownup is the one responsible for deciding what action to take.

c.   *One's own Inner Children's needs take precedence over the needs and wants of outside adults.* The instructions on the airlines emergency cards read, "If you are traveling with a child and the cabin air pressure fails, oxygen masks will drop in front of you. Put your own mask in place first, then put the child's mask in place."

The general rule is, take care of yourself first, and then you will be able to help others as well.

People ask what happens to the Inner Children when the Inner Family is healed. Do they stick around, and does a person get fragmented? Do they grow up or do they go away or disappear? In our experience, they never grow older, but they do heal. They also stick around, but they may seem to disappear because their needs are being met, they don't feel compelled to take over the personality as they used to, and a person's behavior tends to be more appropriate to their chronological age.

In moving through the three phases of Inner Family Healing, there are some basic guidelines we recommend you follow. These are the subject of the next chapter.

3

A Word About Trust

The best piece of advice we can give to facilitate Inner Family Healing is

Trust Your Inner Experience!

That means: **Assume that what you hear or see or feel is valid, even if it doesn't seem to make sense or you think you're making it up.** It may seem very strange indeed to converse with invisible children inside you who can't be proven to exist. Even after completely revamping their lives based on months of conversation with the Inner Children, some clients still question the validity of the Inner Family. We've done it ourselves and you probably will, too. However, that won't significantly interfere with the effectiveness of the process.

If you persist with the Inner Family Healing work, you'll soon be feeling better, and you'll let go of the concern over what the Inner Children are or why the process works, as we have.

The results will speak for themselves. We've learned over the years that when the Inner Children's communications don't seem to make sense to us, it's simply because the Inner Children are referring to things we know nothing about. We can't understand them until we know what they know.

In the meantime, we need to trust that what they're saying is important—sometimes crucially so. For example, a client we'll call Miriam was working on some difficulties she was having in telling people when she was displeased with them. Suddenly, right in the middle of the conversation, she said, "Little Miriam says she was sodomized." Miriam had at the time no conscious memories of any sexual abuse, but as Little Miriam was a three-year-old and wouldn't even have known the meaning of the word, we accepted her statement as significant. Had we allowed anything to interfere with our willingness to believe Little Miriam, we might have blocked the revelation of the severe and prolonged sexual abuse to which she'd been subjected by an uncle, now dead, who was a pillar of society. Today, after months of work on the issue and much prayer, Miriam is largely free of the effects of that abuse. The difference that has made in Miriam's life is extraordinary. No longer does she fear her own sexuality. No longer does she carry rage toward men. No longer does her behavior invite physical harm. No longer does she drive in suicidal ways. She is free to choose what she will do with her life. If she marries, it will be because she freely chooses to, not to prove she's sexually acceptable. If she chooses to remain single, it will be because she prefers it, not because she's paralyzed by indecision or fear. All these freedoms came because she trusted the validity of that one apparently bizarre remark.

Ultimately, any healing process must lead us to embrace ourselves in our entirety—*all* of our Inner Children, not just some of them, our *entire* reality, not merely fragments. To the extent we deny or separate ourselves from any of our Inner Children, we weaken ourselves and, what's more tragic, deprive ourselves of the gifts that every single Inner Child brings to us to make us whole people.

Because self-trust is such an important aspect of Inner Family Healing, being both a means and an end, it's worth taking a moment here to look at the conditioning that leads us to ignore or distort our internal signals.

How We Learn to Mistrust Ourselves

Although we are born trusting ourselves, we are relentlessly conditioned at home and at school to discount our intuition and our emotions. Both men and women are taught to devalue, even despise, their emotions as weakness, their intuition as fantasy or snap judgments, their legitimate perceptions as crazy. We hear things over and over like:

"If you can't hear it, taste it, touch, see, or smell it, it's not real."
"If you can't prove it to someone else, it isn't real."
"The only thing that's real is what can be scientifically proven."
(Those of us who remember when the world was flat and the world was neatly divided into matter and energy know better, of course.)
"What a stupid thing to think! You must be nuts."
"You're not *really* angry at your sister."
"A little thing like that doesn't scare you."

"What do you mean, Uncle Harry touched you? He wouldn't do such a thing."

"You shouldn't feel that way toward anyone."

"What a terrible thing to say! You shouldn't even think those kinds of thoughts."

Those of us who are products of this conditioning tend to believe anyone else before we believe ourselves. This self-doubt makes our lives unnecessarily difficult, robbing us of self-confidence and of the kind of information that makes people function effectively in their personal and work lives. We look to others as authorities, even when it's clear that they aren't, even when it's in their interest to have us at a disadvantage, even when we actually know more about a situation than anyone else. Self-doubt makes us gullible and, worst of all, it makes us indecisive. Some of us are paralyzed by doubt and fear until we absolutely know every factor in a situation, and even then, making a firm decision can be an agony. Some of us hardly ever make a decision; we prefer others to take that responsibility instead, and then we look for evidence to support the wisdom of that preference. "Well, I don't make decisions, because that's how you get clobbered, and things have a way of working themselves out so I really don't have to."

As a society, we've started recognizing the toll that denial and discounting take on the human mind, and things are getting better in some areas. For example, a few schools are beginning to teach that perceptions can be valid even if they can't be confirmed by the five senses or measured in some way.

But progress is slow, and for many of us, these awarenesses and changes come too late to prevent the damage to our self-trust. As adults we still need to do the hard work of reclaiming our own truth.

Some Basic Guidelines for Reclaiming Our Own Truth

People don't learn to trust themselves overnight. We can't. We don't know what to trust and what not to trust. For that reason, it makes sense to enlist the aid of one or more friends whose instincts you respect, who clearly trust their own intuition and act on it successfully. By giving you honest feedback on the validity of your perceptions, they can help you build a body of experience that provides a basis for confidence.

In the therapy room, we serve in that capacity for our clients, and here's what we do.

1. *We affirm repeatedly that everyone has intuition and logic.* Unless you are brain-damaged, you have the capacity to reason, to perceive incongruities between words and actions, to put two and two together and get four. Even if you're dyslexic, you develop compensating mechanisms that can, in the long run, make you even more capable than you might have been without the dysfunction.

    You also have intuition: People seldom manufacture feelings of unease out of nothing at all. We look for the grain of truth in every perception, and we almost inevitably find it.

2. *We provide and invite feedback on specific perceptions.* We also urge clients to share perceptions with others—friends, professional therapists, perhaps a 12-step group, any group made up of people who are themselves on a conscious, positive growth journey. We teach clients how, when they have a sense something is true but aren't sure, to check it out with others. Here's some language for doing so:

    > I need to check out a perception with you. When such and such happened, I got a feeling in my stomach, and I think it means . . . . What's your impression?

    > Did anything strike you as odd about what just happened (and then pause to give them time to think)?

    > I thought such-and-such just happened. Am I seeing things?

    > Such-and-such felt a little strange to me. Is anything going on that you know of?

    Others won't always have the same perceptions, but over a period of time, you, too, can develop some kind of consensual validation for yourself.

3. *We ask people to assign a part of themselves the role of Co-therapist.* We request that they stop us when they think we're off the track. We ask that they offer information they think might be important because the fact they think it's important means it more than likely is. This validates them as experts on their inner world—which is appropriate: we are simply process facilita-

tors, and control of that process remains essentially in their hands.

We also invite clients to own the therapy room's physical space for the time they're there—get up and get themselves a glass of water, a Kleenex—whatever is needed for them to be comfortable. They are full adults, capable of taking responsibility for themselves and getting whatever information is necessary to do so.

4. *We encourage people to write their perceptions down.* Writing often breaks the Family Spell by hooking the Grownup into seeing more clearly.

5. *Most important, we follow the WHEEE principle,* giving full-out acknowledgment for self-trusting behavior, especially when it pays off (which clients tend to overlook)

> **W**ows
> **H**umor
> **E**xcitement
> **E**nthusiasm
> **E**ncouragement, Encouragement,
>   Encouragement, Encouragement

Are you ready to try this? If you're reading for the first time, we suggest you skim the next two chapters. If you're reading it for the second time, it's time to start session one!

4

First Session Instructions

This chapter explains the what, where, when, who, and how of the first session of working with one's Inner Child. It's divided into preparation, process, possible surprises, policies, promises, and presents.

Preparation: What, Where, When, and Who

What the first session is for. The purpose of the first session is to introduce the person to an Inner Child for the first time. Typically, a person meets just one Inner Child in the first session, but it's not unusual for more than one to emerge and we've had as many as six show up.

Who is included. Ideally, the session includes the person, a healing coach (therapist or friend), and a tape recorder to capture the session on tape. We include others in the session only if clients insist.

Where and when to hold the first session. We suggest you choose for your session a quiet place where you are assured of enough time to complete the session uninterrupted, preferably 45 minutes to an hour. Privacy is important. A person should feel free to cry, scream, say whatever is real to them without having to worry about who's going to get upset about what is going on in the session.

Process:
How to Connect With the Inner Children

If you're working with a Healing Coach, agree before beginning the session on a way to signal the Coach that you've caught up to the instructions and are ready for the reading to resume.

You can, of course, simply read the instructions on your own, closing your eyes to do the work and opening them to read what's next.

If you're not working with a Healing Coach, you can also send for our taped version of these instructions, which is available at a nominal charge, or, if you prefer, read this chapter into a tape recorder and play it back to yourself, just as it's written. If that's what you're going to do, don't read the italics aloud—they're separate notes to the Coach, and don't read the numbers—they're just to help you keep your place. Read slowly, in a clear, gentle tone. Where you see three spaced periods (like this . . .), pause for the space of about 20 seconds or until you get a signal from the person to continue. This gives the person time to absorb and follow the instructions.

If you're going to record or be coach, start reading aloud here.

To begin the process, sit comfortably, with arms and legs uncrossed, both feet on the floor, and eyes closed. Take three or four deep breaths, expel each one completely, and let the cares of the day slide off your shoulders. . . .

Check to see if there's anything you need (Kleenex, water, a blanket) . . . If not, we'll go on to the first step.

Now I'm going to ask you to. . .

1. **STIR UP YOUR POSITIVE ENERGY.** Here are some how-to's. Close your eyes for a moment and allow yourself to connect with your gratitude . . . If you aren't currently feeling grateful, think of a time when you did. Even the smallest thing will do . . . Recall what you are grateful for, and the time and place you felt this gratitude . . . Whether or not you were able to capture that feeling of gratitude, don't worry. We're going to move on.

   Next, think of a time when you loved someone or something . . .

   Recreate that feeling, the time, the place . . . You may have beheld a child and wanted to gather that child into your arms to comfort and nurture it . . . If you're having trouble loving a person, think of a time when you loved an object, something soft, or something beautiful. Perhaps when you were little, you held a puppy and saw how trusting and vulnerable it was. Or perhaps you were leaving work and saw an incredible sunset.

Now magnify that feeling, letting it flow throughout your body . . . Just enjoy the sensation . . . That feeling is a faint indication of what you can learn to develop toward your own Inner Children. Take time just to enjoy this feeling. *Note to anyone who cannot connect with feelings of love or gratitude: If you have suffered a recent loss and are grieving, understand that the feelings of love aren't crucial here at this early stage. If you have ever had such feelings and you persist with the process, they will recur.*

*If you cannot remember **ever** having felt love or gratitude, turn to "Magnify the Capacity for Loving," the last heading listed in Chapter 7 (Defusing Inner Sibling Rivalry: The Myth of the Bad Child).*

Now that you're relaxed and energized, we'll go on to the next step . . .

2. **LOCATE THE CHILD.** While keeping the love and gratitude in your awareness, scan through your physical body to see if you can determine where an Inner Child resides. The Child's location may feel younger than the rest of you, or it may feel more emotional, more tender, or perhaps more frightened, excited, tight, or restless. The Inner Child may reside in your eyes, your heart, your tummy, your genitals, the back of your head, even your feet. Sometimes the Inner Child dwells in the arms or the skin. There's actually no place this Child can't or shouldn't reside.

   If you don't have a clear sense of a particular location, think of how you reassure yourself: Do you hold your hands? Your throat? Your stomach? If you're still not sure of a location, don't worry about it. Put your hand on your stomach or heart (there's almost always a Child in one of those two places). Now we'll proceed to the next step.

After you've found the Child, you need to. . .

3. **ACKNOWLEDGE THE CHILD'S PRESENCE.** Acknowledging the Inner Child's presence doesn't mean talking at this point. Rather, it means assuming a mental/emotional attitude toward the Child that expresses your commitment to creating

a bond with the Child regardless of any questions or doubts you may have about the process. It's rather like relating to someone you can't see, but who you know is sitting in a room with you because you saw them before the lights went out.

Now I'm going to ask you to . . .

4. **TOUCH THE CHILD.** When you've selected a part of your body and have acknowledged the Child's presence, take your hand and gently rest it there. (If the Child is between your shoulder blades or another place on the body that's awkward to reach, ask the Child to move to an adjacent area that's easier to reach, the upper arms, for example, and put your hand there, assuming that the Child will move there when ready.)

    Now, recall the loving feeling you had when you thought about the puppy, the rainbow, or the young child, and let it flow out of your heart, up to your shoulder, down your arm and through your hand to the Inner Child. See what kind of touch the Inner Child prefers: Firm? Soft? Stroking? Quiet pressure with the whole hand? Delicate, like a butterfly wing?

Now, once you have made contact,

5. **SPEAK TO THE CHILD WITH LOVE.** You can speak to the Child silently or aloud, whichever works better for you. The main thing is, Be gentle. Remember, you have unwittingly betrayed this young one repeatedly; you've broken promises, you've ignored needs, you've sacrificed in order to cater to someone else, etc. At the least, the Child is unsure of what you'll do. The Child may be angry at you; don't let the anger distract you, however. It doesn't change what the Child wants, and that is a loving, protective, potent Grownup. The Child *wants* to trust you.

Still letting this gentle energy flow, say to the Child

I love you and I'll never, never leave, no matter what happens, as long as you live, and I'll never let you leave me, either.

I'm here to heal old hurts and to learn to love and care for you the way you need and want to be cared for. My job is to give you everything you need and most of what you want.

6. **ASK IF THE CHILD BELIEVES YOU.** Listen for the answer and trust that what you get in response is actually what the Child is telling you. The response may be in the form of a feeling, a thought, an image, or a sensation. Sometimes you'll find your eyes filling with tears—that usually is your Child crying in relief. Abandonment and isolation are terrors for all Children, and hearing that they won't be abandoned meets a deep need. (If the Child believes the Grownup, go to Step 7.)

   If the Inner Child doubts you, it's because of some previous abandonment, reinforced by your own neglect. If the Child is silent, that means its answer is no. Here's how to respond:

   a. Tell the Child it's fine to distrust you—after being badly hurt, a person needs time to be sure your word is worth something. Trust, once broken, must be earned back.
   b. Say that you *can't* leave this Child even if you wanted to. Because you inhabit the same physical body, you will be with them for as long as they live.
   c. Admit that although you haven't abandoned the Child physically, you *have* left emotionally and mentally.
   d. Say that you are truly sorry for the pain that caused, and you hope they will forgive you.

      Ask if the Child is willing to forgive you.

      If the Child is not yet willing to forgive, say you understand, and that you intend to earn their trust through assuming full responsibility as a Grownup, listening, protecting, learning, and loving.

      If the Child forgives you, be aware that forgiveness will be an ongoing process. Forgiving you now is an expression of the Child's intent. But before the process is complete, the Child may need to express anger or pain regarding many specific wrongs and let go of them individually.

Next,

7. **ASK THE INNER CHILD FOR MORE INFORMATION.** Ask the Child what name he or she wants to be called. (If there's no answer, don't worry. If you don't hear it now, the Child will likely tell you later.)
   — See if you can picture this Child. How old is this Child?
   — What does the Child like to do?
   — How is the Child feeling about this conversation?

— Is there anything the Child wants you to know? wants to tell you? wants to ask?

We've done a lot now, so . . .

8. **LET YOUR INNER CHILD KNOW YOU'RE GOING TO FINISH THIS PARTICULAR CONVERSATION.** Say, "I'm going to stop talking to you shortly and do something else for a while. But before I do,
   a. "Is there anything else you'd like to say to me? . . .
   b. "I, your Grownup, want to give you a gift. What would you like to have from me?" The Child may want a trip to the zoo, a cuddly animal. Whatever the Child wants, give it—either in fantasy now, or reality later. If possible, give the gift in reality.
   c. "Remember, I love you very much, and I'll never leave you, no matter what.
   d. "Thank you for trusting me enough to talk to me. It took great courage, and I appreciate that very much.
   e. "I will be communicating with you again. When would you like me to talk with you again? I'll also choose when to speak with you, but I'd like to know what *you'd* like."

Be sure to leave the Child in a comfortable situation, properly supervised—playing outside, resting, whatever is suitable to the Child's age and need at the moment.

We recommend you write down which Inner Children you met, their names, age, gender, location, fears, likes & dislikes, promises, what you did, and what they did. It may seem vivid now, but as time goes on, your memory may get a little blurry.

The first meeting with any Inner Child needs to cover all the items in this basic format. The following dialogue illustrates a very typical first session conversation with an Inner Child who is just being discovered.

Coach: Before we begin, I just want to say to you that there are two therapists in this room. You and I are going to be co-therapists. I may know more about this process than you do, but nobody knows more about what's going on inside your Inner Family than you. If I get stuck, I'm going to call Time Out so we can work out together where to go next. Sometimes I'll be asking you if you see anything that I'm missing, or if something I'm doing is bothering you. Is that OK with you?

Client: Well, I'm not sure how good a therapist I am, but if it suits you, it's OK with me.

Coach: Good. Now close your eyes and take three or four deep breaths, deep enough to expel the week-old air in the bottom of your lungs. Let tension slide off your shoulders and melt into the floor. Now, fill your body with a beautiful blue, the deep, clear, sparkling blue of the Caribbean. Let it wash every fiber, bone, hair, and joint, fresh and cool. Now, very gently begin pouring in through the top of your head liquid sunshine, golden and brilliant, warm and healing. There's a straight line across where the two colors meet. Let that line move down your body, taking about two minutes from head to toe.

Client: (breathes deeply and exhales with relief.) I feel very relaxed now.

Coach: Now it's time to stir up your positive energy: Remember a time when you felt grateful for something . . . Now remember a time when you loved something or someone . . . Now let that feeling expand in your heart and flow out your arms and into your hands. You may even feel your hands tingle pleasantly . . . (Client nods)

 Next, scan through your body again and see if there's a part that feels younger than the rest, more vulnerable, maybe more emotional.

Client: I feel some pain in my stomach. It's where I get tense whenever I have a big meeting coming up.

Coach: Good. Put your hand there and see what kind of touch feels best. A warm firm pressure? or stroking?

Client: Just a warm pressure.

Coach: Fine. Now that sensation is a signal your Inner Child is giving you, so you know that your stomach is where that Inner Child resides. Take a moment to think about that, and realize there's a young person waiting to speak to you. Now say to the Child, "I love you and, no matter what happens, I'm never leaving you, and I'm never letting you leave me either."

Client: (to the Inner Child) I love you and no matter what happens, I'm never leaving you. (Starts to cry)

Coach: What's the Inner Child's response?

Client: She's waited to hear those words for so long.

Coach: Right. When we've waited for something so long, sometimes when it finally arrives, there's a whole backlog of tears for all the time we didn't get it. It's fine to cry, and since you and the Grownup only have one body to share, she'll have to use your body to do her crying. But be aware that you are also the Grownup and you need to stay aware that you are an adult responsible for this little one.

Client: She's been very lonely.

Coach: Tell her she never has to be lonely again. Tell her you're here to learn to love and care for her the way she needs and wants to be cared for. Tell her she can always come to you, and you'll be with her to comfort her and to play with her.

Client: (To her Inner Child) You never have to be lonely again. Just come to me any time, and I'll comfort you and play with you. We'll have a good time. I'm learning to give you what you need and want, because I'm committed to being a good Grownup for you.

Coach: Does she believe you?

Client: No. She'd like to, but she's afraid that when I have work to do, I'll neglect her like I always have.

Coach: Tell her that there will be times when you'll need to be working and can't play with her right that minute, but that she can come to you and sit next to you or in your lap while you work. If that's not possible either, you'll put your hand where she is, on your stomach, until she feels better, and you'll make a date to talk with her just as soon as you can.

Client: She heard that and says it would be OK. But she still doesn't really believe that I'll do what I say I'll do. She's not saying it out loud, but I can tell.

Coach: She's really smart, and she's right. Tell her that you're just learning some new habits, and you probably *will* forget and go back to old habits from time to time. It takes time to install new ways of doing things, but you're absolutely committed to this learning, so you'll be getting better and better at it. . . .

Client: (to the Inner Child) Sweetheart, I don't blame you for not trusting me. You're right, I probably will let you down, because I'm not used to hearing you when you need me. But I promise you, I will get better, and you'll know by my behavior when that happens.

Coach: In the meantime, tell her it's fine for her to distrust you. You've earned her distrust by letting her down many, many times. In fact, say to her that you regret those times very much, and you want her to know you're sorry. Ask her if she's willing to forgive you and to be patient while you're learning.

Client: Sweetheart, it's OK to be careful about trusting me. I haven't been much of a parent to you, and for that I'm very, very sorry. Will you forgive me? (starts to cry again) I didn't even finish before she was saying yes, yes, and she's hugging me.

Coach: That's wonderful. She's a beautiful Child, with a beautiful, generous, forgiving heart. Ask her what her name is.

Client: Clarice? I don't know anyone named Clarice!

Coach: It doesn't matter, that's her name. And if it isn't, she'll let us know later. What does Clarice look like?

Client: She's about three, and she has long hair.

Coach: Is there anything the Child wants you to know? For example, what does she like to do?

Client: She likes to play with puppies and kittens and she likes hugging and she likes eating ice cream.

Coach: Neat. Is there anything else she would like you to know?

Client: (to the Inner Child) Is there anything else you want me to know? No, not right now.

Coach: Tell her you're going to conclude this conversation in a couple of minutes, but before you do, you want to give her a present. Ask her what she'd like for a present.

Client: (to the Inner Child) I'm going to stop talking with you in a little bit, but I'd like to give you a nice present before I do. What would you like me to give you? She wants a puppy all her own.

Coach: What kind?

Client: I can see it. It's a beautiful little golden cocker spaniel.

Coach: So give her that right now. And also, tell her that this is all hers for as long as she lives.

Client: She's going to name it Goldie. She's hugging the puppy, and she's very happy.

Coach: Is there anything else she wants or needs?

Client: No. Yes, a hug. I'm hugging her now. I feel really good about her, and about giving her Goldie.

Coach: Tell her you want to hear whenever she needs anything, and ask her if she's willing to get your attention when she needs something.

Client: (to the Inner Child) Will you tell me when you need something? I want to hear what you need. . . . . She says yes. She wants a soft, stuffed bunny to hug.

Coach: Wow. She's really asking for what she wants! That's wonderful. Are you willing to give her a stuffed bunny?

Client: Oh, yes. I'd love to get her a bunny.

Coach: Good. Tell her.

Client: Clarice, I will buy you a white bunny on Monday. I promise.

Coach: Now, before you sign off with Clarice, think about how many times you would be willing to speak with her throughout the day.

Client: I could talk to her at the beginning and the end, and when I go to the ladies room before lunch. I could probably do more.

Coach: Three times as a first promise is probably plenty. And you can do more if that works. So tell her you promise to speak with her at least three times a day plus any time she calls for your attention.

Client: I promise to speak with you when I get up and when I go to bed and before I go to lunch every day, Clarice. And if I forget, or if you want my attention more than that, I want you to let me know, and I promise to pay attention if I'm aware.

Coach: Are you expecting her to do the reminding if you forget?

Client: Sure, that would be great.

Coach: I'm calling Time Out. I need to talk with my co-therapist. . . . Is my co-therapist present?

Client: Yes.

Coach: There's a danger here I want to let you know about. Without realizing it, the Grownup is actually asking the Inner Child to share responsibility for the Grownup doing her job. It's very important that she not do that. Remembering is the Grownup's job, and she needs to take full responsibility for it. Do you follow me?

Client: Absolutely. The Grownup needs to get an alarm watch or write herself notes or whatever she has to to remember. I hear you loud and clear. (to the Inner Child) Clarice, thank you for being willing to remind me of my responsibilities, but I'll handle that. What I will ask you to do is let me know when you need something or you're upset. Is that OK by you? . . . She feels better about that than before. She was a little upset but didn't want me to know.

Not every session goes this smoothly. Inner Children are just as varied as outer children. Here are some of the surprises that may await you.

Possible Surprises

We have learned to accept whatever the client presents as valid, even when it doesn't seem to make sense to us at the time. We go with it, helping the Grownup to draw out the Inner Child's thoughts and feelings until some resolution has been reached. Again and again, the results confirm that trusting the Inner Children's information works, whether we're dealing with opposite gender children, other types of historical facts that don't fit the person's actual life, or inner monsters.

For example, about 30 percent of our clients find one or more Inner Children who are of a different gender from their own. This has nothing to do with homosexuality: The majority of those clients in whom we've seen different-gender Inner Children have been heterosexual. So what could account for it?

One possible explanation for the existence of these opposite gender Inner Children is that they represent efforts to cope with our society's nonsensical insistence on defining both females and males as less than fully human. We say that women are sensitive and emotional while men never feel pain and don't need to cry; that women are intuitive and men are logical; that women are submissive and weak and men are dominant and powerful—*real* men, that is. The truth is, men are leaders *and* followers; dominant *and* submissive; tender *and* tough; intuitive, deeply feeling, *and* logical; powerful *and* weak. So are women. But because of the way our society looks at it, most little boys and girls are "socialized" into believing they must cut off a part of who they are to be acceptable as the gender they are.

- Peter, sensitive as a boy, decided his tender self wasn't male enough and split those qualities off into another Inner Child, a girl, who he then denied and put down, while continuing to develop outwardly along the lines of what society calls "male." This left him with an unacknowledged tenderness that he had no skills to express. When he came to us, we educated his Grownup: (a) to love this Inner Girl and encourage her to express herself to him; (b) to realize she is a source of strength, not weakness; and (c) to develop the skills needed to express that strength.

  Invariably, following this route has heightened men's self-acceptance and enhanced their ability to connect with others.

- Another client, Cathy, who was outspoken and athletic as a girl, saw that her more timid mother and her dominating father regarded her strength as unseemly for "a nice Southern girl." At that point, she split herself into an aggressive Inner Boy and a more submissive Inner Girl and arrested the development of her assertive self. She came to us because she found it difficult to express her power: her tendency was to flip from aggression to passivity to covert manipulation. As she reacquaints herself with her Inner Boy and the associated characteristics she has reserved to him, she is developing the skills to express her power and drive in a graceful way.

Here's another kind of surprise, in this case also related to having opposite gender children. Sometimes an Inner Child will report a traumatic event that it is certain never happened to that person. One man, for example, found a 3 year old Inner Girl who reported being severely and frequently molested by a man who does not exist in our client's own history. In conventional terms, this made no sense, but as you'll see, it was absolutely crucial to go with it anyway. Once the Grownup established a proper relationship with this Inner Child, the person was able to drop drugs, alcohol, and sugar within a matter of weeks. As of this writing, almost two years later, the person is functioning at exceptional levels in school, work, interpersonal relationships, self care, and spiritually.

Given results like these, you can see why we willingly let factual accuracy take a back seat to the therapeutic process. The event may represent something else that did happen, just as dreams symbolically express other events occurring in our lives. Or it may represent something that happened to a parent or sibling that the Inner Child has taken on in an effort to help that person. Or it may be a fantasy. Regardless what the real story may be, straightening out the relationship between the Grownup and the Inner Children is what produces results. When we take the Inner Children's stories as true and help the person work through all the associated thoughts and feelings, dysfunctions clear up.

One surprise that we don't take as true is Inner Monsters. People commonly report having a monster inside them that all the Inner Children fear, and we confront that with no hesitancy. Inner Children are never monsters, although they may present themselves as such, much as the Wizard of Oz made himself sound like a scary giant. We urge the Grownup to find the real Inner Child, to see how old it is, and not to allow it to hide on a permanent basis. Then we go through the same steps as we do for any Inner Child. Here's an example:

Client: There's a monster here, and all the kids are scared of it. So am I. I don't want to deal with it.

Coach: That's no monster, that's an Inner Child. What kind of monster face is it putting on?

Client: It's really big and really mean, and it's got teeth and claws, like a dinosaur. The other Inner Kids are scared.

Coach: What a creative kid! Tell that Inner Child that you're not fooled, although you were for a while, and that you want him to come out and show the real person. Is it a boy or a girl?

Client: He says, "No, you can't make me." And I don't want to try.

Coach: Oh, so it's a boy. Where's the Grownup? Stand up and make sure you are feeling your physical strength. . . . That's better.

Tell him you love him, that you'll never leave him, and you'll never, ever give up on him, no matter what . . . Now, tell him you're not about to let him fool and scare everybody. Run after him and keep holding him until he stops fighting. It doesn't matter how much he yells and screams and kicks. You're bigger and you're stronger, and if you hang in there, he'll get worn out.

Client: I'm holding onto him, but I'm exhausted. I can't hold on any more.

Coach: What's happening now?

Client: It was a standoff. We're both wiped out, lying down on the ground.

Coach: Good. Now go over to him and tell him how glad you are that he was willing to show himself to you. How happy you are that he's so strong. That now you will be loving him and learning to take care of him as you've never done before. Ask him if he'd like to rest with you a while, maybe in your lap.

Client: He's willing to lean against me.

Coach: That's nice. How old is he?

Client: About seven.

Coach: He'll get into hugging later. You know, all children want hugs, even if they're scared. And all Inner Children want to have an Inner Grownup in charge, even if they say they don't. It just takes time to build the trust. How are the rest of the Children doing?

Client: They're happy that I turned out to be so strong, but they still don't trust him, and they don't know what will happen next time.

Coach: That's OK. Tell them that you're going to be staying on the job, and they don't have to worry about protecting themselves from this little one. They'll find out how true that is as time goes on.

For much younger Inner Children who appear as monstrous, we allow more space. For example, we have the Grownup tell such Inner Children they can stay hidden where they are for a while if they're willing to have a conversation. They can come out when they're ready. If they're really tiny, infancy or pre-birth, they won't have words to speak with, but they'll communicate through emotions. (Pre-birth children need to know, by the way, they need not come out at all.)

Policies

In working with clients, we adhere to two policies that we recommend you consider adopting for yourself. One is the no-suicide contract. The other is an agreement to suspend any substance abuse or other serious addiction and do whatever is required to support yourself in carrying out that agreement.

The No-Suicide Contract

Very few of the people we work with are truly suicide risks, but many of our clients have a strong thought that if things get bad enough, they can always kill themselves, either accidentally or deliberately. Keeping that option open robs them of some or all of the strength they need in order to make their lives good enough to keep on living. It's like having a hole in the bucket.

We make a no-suicide contract whenever we encounter an Inner Child who is depressed, hopeless, or deeply angry, especially if the person has had a great loss recently. If the person resists, we say, truthfully, that we aren't willing to work with someone who refuses to agree to stay alive to the end of the treatment. Here's the no-suicide contract:

> **I will not hurt or kill myself,**
> **or let anyone else hurt or kill me,**
> **accidentally or on purpose,**
> **no matter what.**

We also ask the client what the loophole is and how the Inner Children would sabotage the contract. That contract needs to be made between the Grownup of the depressed person and another human being. If the client won't make it for life, then we make the contract for a definite period of time with a provision that it stays in effect until the person has spoken with us. We say, however, that as far as we're concerned, the contract is forever.

Staying Sober and Legal

We will not work with anyone who is actively using drugs and/or alcohol or persisting in any activity that is illegal. Therapy is virtually useless in our experience unless the person is willing to do whatever they have to do to remain sober. "Whatever-they-have-to-do" may include going to Alcoholics Anonymous, Debtors Anonymous, Narcotics Anonymous, or any number of other 12-step programs. Active drunks, addicts, and abusers can't begin to keep promises, which is what Inner Family Healing is built on.

Promises

We ask everyone we work with to make promises to their Inner Children. Keeping those promises comprises a crucial part of building trust in the Inner Children and a sense of potency in the Grownup. We inform the Grownup that the Inner Children lose trust in the Grownup for good reason, and that the Grownup's job in the process is to *earn* back that trust. It's not realistic to expect Inner Children who've been betrayed again and again to become trusting overnight. It is appropriate for the Grownup to *earn* their trust, little by little.

The kinds of things people make promises about range from communicating with their Inner Children, to giving them gifts, to taking time off from work for playing, to following through on some other commitments. These commitments can be very important. For example, someone who hasn't done their taxes for a number of years is subjecting their Inner Children to enormous emotional and physical strain and anxiety—every kid over a certain age knows there's a time to pay the piper. In such a situation, one might promise to hire a tax person to begin clearing up one's finances as a way to protect and care for the Inner Children.

Of all the promises, perhaps the most important over the long term is the promise to communicate. We ask the person how many times per day they would be willing to promise to speak with each Inner Child to convey love and to discover and meet their other needs. We suggest communicating at least twice a day for 2 to 5 minutes. Good times for such communication include before getting out of bed in the morning, driving or riding to or from work or anywhere else, moments in the bathroom, and just before going to sleep. Here's how to do the communicating:

1. Take a few deep breaths, letting the tension slide off your shoulders and onto the floor. Look through your body and, wherever you find tense muscles, breathe air and sunlight into the tense area. Then imagine yourself breathing cobwebs and tension out.

2. Place your hand where an Inner Child resides and acknowledge his or her presence with a "Hello, I'm here." Then give them the following messages.

    I love you.

    You're safe.

    I'm never leaving you.

    I want you to tell me if there's anything you need or want from me right now. What do you need?

    I want to know what you think. What are you thinking?

    I want to know what you feel. What are you feeling now?

3. Do this for each of the Inner Children. If you're in a hurry, you may not have time to listen for responses to all the questions, but you can give each of the Inner Children a hug and promise to get back to them later.

Inner Children can always tell when they're being treated with respect, so in communicating with them, the Grownup must be truly open, truly listening. It's especially important not to patronize or try to pacify them. Here's Miriam's account of her discovering the difference between listening and pacifying:

I remember riding home from work on the bus, a long ride of 30 to 40 minutes. I was feeling tension in my diaphragm, which is where my three-year-old is located. I wasn't really upset, but I was aware of her presence. So I decided to talk to her the way Mary had suggested. I put my hand on my diaphragm and asked her, What's wrong? You can tell me, kid." There was no answer. I stayed with it for a while, but still she didn't reply.

Walking home from the bus stop a few minutes later, with no results, I realized that although the words I said were OK, my manner had replicated that of my over-stressed parents. "Hurry up kid and tell me, I'm getting tired" was about what I was communicating.

I stopped walking, asked her forgiveness for treating her like that, and told her I was really glad she was within me, and I really loved her. All at once, I had a flash of her face peeking at me from around a corner with a huge smile on her face. It was great! It was great!

As this example illustrates, when the Inner Children won't respond, it's often because where the Grownup is coming from fails to honor them as human beings with dignity.

In making promises to Inner Children who are too young to talk, it's often appropriate to promise to hold them with you all the time. To do so, fashion in your imagination a Snugli—that's a strong, soft-cloth sling that you wrap around yourself to keep a baby close to your heart. Use imagination (we use Alice-in-Wonderland magic drops) to make the Inner Child small enough to fit into the Snugli. When they want to be their own size again, we administer Alice's antidote drops. If you use this technique, keep checking in periodically to make sure the baby is still content with you; if not, find out the need and meet it. This may sound silly to you, but in our experience, the results have been dramatic. Snuglis can also be useful for an older Inner Child, especially one who has been tantruming.

Presents

Not only are presents very important to children, they remain important to our Inner Children as we mature. Consider the stories of parents who buy presents that are ostensibly for their children but are obviously for themselves: A father, very poor as a child, went out when he became rich to buy his son a train set for his first birthday; years later, the father still won't let his son play with the trains without him. We've known a mother to buy her daughter a beautiful doll and then tend to the doll's clothes and hair herself—letting her daughter play with the doll only if her hands are clean, and then only for a short period of time under her watchful eye.

We've made it a regular part of our practice to give gifts, like stuffed animals, dolls, pillows, and toys. Doing so serves three main purposes.

First, giving gifts models generosity the person needs to learn to show toward his or her own Inner Children. Whether the person plays with the toys or not doesn't matter. The fact that they are there gives visual pleasure, reminds the person—both the Grownup and the Inner Children—that love is flowing in their direction, and creates a positive climate that contributes to the healing of memories.

Second, the gift provides concrete evidence of affection and friendship. This helps the person to begin building trust.

Finally, giving gifts offers an opportunity for creating fun and pleasure, an important skill in loving oneself and enjoying life.

Giving stuffed animals and dolls seems to be especially helpful to women. Having and hugging a doll who represents an Inner Child of theirs seems to open them to loving the Inner Child more. Women whose professional lives take them all over the country have traveled with the dolls they've received. Men are more reluctant to accept dolls, but they gladly receive a stuffed animal, for example, a little bear. In each case, the person's choice to keep the doll or toy close testifies to the power of such a gift to move the Inner Child. Here's an illustration.

> Joe was one of the people we worked with informally very early on. He was a very lonely man. He was in his forties, divorced, and alienated from his children. In the course of the years, he shared with us about his deprived, abused, unloving childhood. He may have been raised by his mother, as he never mentioned his father. We gave him a little rock one evening, just as a reminder of our affection for him. A while later, after another meeting, we did a brief exercise with him out in the street and he got in touch with "Little Joey." Before we parted, he pulled out his rock and showed it to us—all polished and loved. A few weeks later, he proudly said he had bought a new stereo for "Little Joey." We said, "That's great for the teenage Joe, but not for the little one. What does *Little* Joey want?" The reply that came was "A red fire engine." He couldn't find anything like a red fire engine, but the following week he bought a red car for himself. He was very happy, but again, we told him, this was more for the teenager. A few weeks later, we found and gave Joe a tiny red fire engine, and suddenly he understood that he had been avoiding loving "Little Joey" just the way his mother had when he was young. When he realized this, he was appalled and swore he'd never treat himself badly again or allow anyone else to do so either. He no longer retains employees who were abusive, and he has dropped those acquaintances who were using him. Facing up to the realities wasn't easy, but his life has since expanded to include people who truly care for him, and he is immeasurably happier.

Of course, the ultimate aim of these presents is to teach the Grownup to give gifts to its own Inner Children, as one expression of loving them. Ideally, the person will go out and purchase their own present. We suggest to the person that the Grownup take the Inner Children to the store, allow an Inner Child to pick the toy or doll it wants, and buy it. We urge clients not to worry about the cost—there are places and times to save pennies, but this isn't one of them. Even if the toy the Inner Child wants is expensive, the investment is a good one. The Inner Children are worth it!

5

What To Do in the Second and Succeeding Sessions

Usually everyone's first session can be assumed to run along similar lines. It's after you have met the Inner Children and begun to deal with their specific needs that sessions differ significantly. Chapters 6 through 9 are designed to give you as much information as possible to enable you to deal with those more individual matters, but we can give a few guidelines to help you handle the continuing relationship with your Inner Children. We've organized these guidelines in two main sections: (1) instructions for the second session; and (2) later sessions.

Instructions for the Second Session

On the premise that building trust between Inner Children and the Grownup is the number one priority, the principal work of the second session—and all early sessions—begins with following up on the promises made to the Inner Children in the preceding session. This format needs to be followed for as long as it takes the Grownup to assume its responsibilities.

These instructions focus particularly on the promises regarding communicating, but the same basic format applies for any other kinds of promises, e.g., buying a stuffed animal or toy, taking a trip, taking time off from work, or doing taxes.

So the first question to ask the Grownup is, *Have you kept your promise to the Inner Child?* If the Grownup has kept the promise made in session one regarding communicating, you will have touched and conversed with the Inner Child at least once a day since. If you *have* communicated with the Inner Children, then the questions under "If the Grownup Has Kept Promises" will serve to guide the session. If you have *not* communicated with the Inner Children, then use the material included under the heading, "If the Grownup Has Broken Promises." Regardless of which section applies, do read the entire chapter.

If the Grownup Has Kept Promises

If you have communicated with your Inner Children daily since the last session, then ask these questions:

1. *What have you said to your Inner Children and how?* Think about the following options for communicating with the Inner Children and see if there are any you overlooked that sound like they'd be particularly useful to you.
   Touch the Inner Children.
   Speak aloud, hum, or sing.
   Speak silently.
   Write a letter.
   Write down the responses.

2. *How did your Inner Child respond?* There's no "right" response, by the way, so don't try to be right. Inner Children are very independent and original, so you can be sure that whatever response you get will contain some surprises.
   If the Inner Children didn't seem to respond, be aware that ***whatever*** *happens is a response. The Inner Children have been listening, and you can count on that.* The Grownup's job is just to keep talking and listening. *Eventually the Children will respond noticeably because they want to.*

3. *Have you noticed anything that's different about your life since the last session?* There's almost always something. If nothing else, some people may report needing additional sleep. During the early phases of Inner Family Healing, deep work can require up to 2 hours additional sleep a night. If you notice nothing different, go on to the next question.

4. *Have you had any nurturing lately? especially any nurturing touch?* The Inner Family Healing process can be quite stressful, and you may feel younger and more vulnerable than usual. Are you

getting enough physical touch? If not, consider hiring a professional massage therapist at least every other week.

5. *How do you feel about the process?* You may be ambivalent,
   frightened, skeptical, angry. Everyone who's been through the
   process has felt these feelings, because, if nothing else, some of
   the Inner Children are upset by the prospect of change or
   discovery. All feelings are OK and should be voiced so they can
   be released.

6. *What's on your mind today?* This is always a good question to ask
   to see how the Family Spell is operating or weakening. Often
   the answer reveals an incident that offers an opportunity to heal
   a pattern between the Grownup and one of the Inner Children.

Here's an example of a person, Helga, whose Grownup is well-developed in some areas but underdeveloped in others. When she first received
information about taking care of her Inner Children, her Grownup immediately went to work, learning what she needed to learn and practicing
new skills.

I used to think that feeling like a child was immature (and therefore
bad) behavior on my part, and that I needed to work harder at
being a mature adult. Working harder meant trying to play the role
of a mature person and act as if everything was all right emotionally. But the harder I worked, the worse I felt.

Then I attended a renewal workshop at which Jacqui Bishop
spoke. After her talk, Jacqui sat with me and I told her about some
of the problems I was having. She asked me if I had ever worked
with my Inner Children. As we talked, there arose a familiar feeling
of tension in my midsection, and I placed my hand on my abdomen
where I was feeling discomfort and anxiety. Jacqui asked me where
my Inner Child was located, and instinctively I said, "Right here in
my abdomen, beneath my hand." Jacqui went on to explain that
we all have Inner Children who need to be nurtured or parented
and who communicate their discomfort to us when their needs are
not being met. She said it is not only *not* a lack of maturity when
they make their needs known, but that our first and foremost
obligation is to take care of them, to recognize, acknowledge and
communicate with them and to meet their needs. Then and only
then can we really grow and grow up.

That day I felt that together we had turned a new page in my book of life. I felt that we had hit on the key to my future health and happiness.

In the weeks that followed, as I became more aware of my Inner Child, Julie, and more cognizant of her specific needs, I became more open to my own feelings. But I had difficulty making the move from being aware of Julie's fears and anxieties to being able to speak to her in a meaningful way. I spoke to Jacqui about it, and she simply asked me, "How would you speak to Andy (my nine-year-old son) if he expressed the same feelings to you?" Well, that did it! I have very strong and healthy parenting instincts toward my son, and I began applying them to Julie.

Whenever Julie's fear manifested itself in that stomach ache that was so familiar, I asked her what she was afraid of. Generally a specific fear would surface within me, and I would begin talking to her. For example, I would say, "Honey, I know you are afraid of going into that meeting with Mr. so-and-so, but you must come along with me. However, I will be there with you the whole time, and I won't allow anyone to mistreat you." As I spoke to her, I held her in that part of my body where she and the feeling were located. Then, after making this commitment to her, I would go to the meeting and there, whenever I could, I reassured Little Julie in my mind. And if I felt there was something she needed protection from (harsh words, for example), I came to her—and my—defense in an adult manner and/or exited the situation, also in an adult manner. Having made the commitment to protect her, I somehow mustered up the strength to do so. And the more I was able to nurture Julie, the stronger I became as an adult.

Later Jacqui informed me I don't have to bring Julie to my business meetings. Children don't need to participate in Grownup business decisions, she said, and it's quite acceptable to leave them home to play in a safe situation. So now I tell Julie I'm going to an adult meeting, I ask her if there's anything she needs before I go, and I say that when I return I'll tell her all about it if she wants to hear. She feels a lot better that way, and so do I.

If the Grownup Has Broken Promises

It's very common for the Grownup to break promises in the early stage of Inner Family Healing. Some of us block awareness of our Inner Child's feelings and needs for years, distracting ourselves with mental or physical activity of some kind. Don't be surprised if, having made a promise to take care of the Inner Children's needs, you utterly ignore them in the early stages. Creating new patterns takes intention, practice, and more practice.

Don't come down hard on anyone for breaking the promise—yourself, the Grownup, or the Inner Children. That is abuse, which never did work. Have some compassion for these young persons, both the one who wants to abuse and the one who is feeling abused. Remember what they've been through and you'll find it easier to forgive them and yourself for being human. Instead, aim toward restored communication and caring between the Grownup and the Inner Children and commit to new promises. Here's a series of questions to guide you in doing that:

1. *How do you, the Grownup, feel about having broken your promises?* Common feelings are: ashamed, scared of being incompetent, angry and trying to blame something or someone else, defensive, indifferent.

    None of these feelings in and of themselves are good or bad. The important thing is to be open about the feelings, to work through them, and to find the love and compassion for the Inner Children that lies beneath them.

    Remember, wounded Inner Children *want* to trust the Grownup, and **it's honesty, not perfection, that lays the foundation for that trust.**

2. *How do the Inner Children feel?* Some of the feelings mentioned above may come from an Inner Child, especially if there's a lot of resentment.

3. *Are you willing to make a new promise?* If so go to question #4. If you are not willing to make a new promise, you will not have to walk the plank. The "Grownup" may not be a Grownup at all, but another Inner Child instead. Go to Section C—and meet the Inner Child masquerading as a Grownup.

4. *What are you willing to promise?* It's important, in light of the difficulty of keeping the first promise, to make sure that the new promise is reasonable. It might make sense to make a promise for a shorter time period than before, or to do things that require less time and effort, and to create a memory system—notes to yourself, an alarm watch, or other trigger.

5. *Are you willing to ask the Inner Children's forgiveness?* (In some circles it's called eating humble pie.) If the Grownup is in

charge, then ultimately the willingness to apologize will be there. If not, read chapter 9, which may clear up any misunderstanding regarding what apology and forgiveness are about.

In apologizing, say you feel bad about having let the Inner Children down, and you're truly sorry. It's no excuse, but explain that you're learning and it's going to take you some time. Ask them to forgive you and give you another chance.

If the Inner Children are willing to forgive, fine. If not, make a new promise and stick to it. And keep doing so until you've proven yourself trustworthy.

In the following dialogue sample, you'll see how following up on promises helps educate the Grownup in responsible parenting. You'll also see how Inner Children keep showing up and what to do about it.

Coach: Did you keep your promises to the Inner Children?

Client: I bought the bunny, but I just couldn't talk with my Inner Children.

Coach: What happened?

Client: It was boring. Nothing happened.

Coach: What did you do?

Client: Well, I looked for them and they weren't there. Then I tried to say I love you, but it felt stupid, so I gave up after a few times.

Coach: How do you feel about that?

Client: Not wonderful. I should have done better—after all, it was only 2 or 3 minutes three times a day. But a lot of thoughts come up suggesting this is a dumb process that doesn't really work, and it's expensive. And I feel a little angry at the Children—if they're there, that is.

Coach: Good! You're right on track. (Client looks amazed.)

First of all, congratulations for even remembering to pay attention to your Inner Children. A lot of people forget completely. So you're a step ahead.

Second, you remembered to buy the gift. That's great. Do you like the bunny you bought?

Client: Yeah. It's really big and soft.

Coach: That's great. Third, even though you have doubts about the Inner Children's existence, you're angry at them for not showing up. That indicates you're relating to them, even if it's angrily right this moment.

Client: I never thought of it that way. Actually, I left something out. I feel a little bad for not sticking with it.

Coach: So that's another plus. You actually regret not having kept your promises to them. That's appropriate, get it? You're actually doing and feeling some appropriate things for a good Grownup to do and feel.

Now, let me give you some information about keeping promises. The Grownup was the one who promised to do something. The Inner Children are always there, even if you can't tell, but they didn't promise to communicate with the Grownup. So the Grownup is the only one who needs to keep a promise.

And here's your promise: to speak lovingly, to ask about needs, and to listen for responses. If the Inner Children don't respond, don't worry about it. You can absolutely rely on the fact that the Inner Children want a functioning Grownup, and if you prove your trustworthiness to them over a period of time, they'll show up. Do you understand what I'm saying?

Client: Yes. You're saying that I should keep talking and listening no matter what comes back. That the kids want an Inner Grownup, and at a certain point, they'll decide to take the risk of trusting me, and then they'll communicate freely.

Coach: Right. You also need to let the Inner Children know that you will make mistakes. You're not perfect and you're just learning. Tell them that and see if that's OK with them.

Client: (Communicates silently with Inner Children.) They say it's OK, as long as I don't try to blame my mistakes on them.

Coach: Terrific. So what are you willing to promise for the next time?

Client: The same thing: Talk to them and listen for at least 2 minutes, three times a day.

Coach: And if you fail to do that in any given day?

Client: I'll go to the Inner Children as soon as I'm aware and say to them how sorry I am and spend some extra time to help show them I'm sincere.

Coach: Terrific!

Client: Wait a minute. Something's going on. I'm starting to feel really angry. I think there's another Child in here.

Coach: Great. Where in your body is this Inner Child?

Client: In my eyes.

Coach: So take your hand and put it where this Inner Child is. Is it a girl or a boy?

Client: It's another girl. Now I'm getting a headache.

Coach: Thank her for coming to introduce herself. Tell her she doesn't have to give you a headache to get your attention. You're happy to talk with her. Ask her what she's angry about.

Client: She says Clarice gets all the attention and besides she says Clarice is stupid.

Coach: How old is this Child?

Client: About nine. She's really mad.

Coach: See what she looks like, and find out what her name is.

Client: She's got her hands on her hips and she's just covered with dirt. She's a real tomboy. I can't even tell what color her hair is! (to the Inner Child) What's your name? She says her name is Spit.

Coach: Naw—that's not her real name. Nobody names a child Spit. She's just saying that because she's so spitting mad. I think she needs a bath. Why don't you give her a bath.

Client: She's running away.

Coach: Well, you can catch her. Actually, kids really want to be given safe limits. They want you to tell them what they can and can't do, so they can learn how to take good care of themselves. They also, by the time they get to her age, like to wrestle. So you may be in for a sprint and a wrestling match.

Client: I've caught her and we're rolling around on the ground. She's really hard to hold onto. . . . Now I've got her into a huge hot tub with lots of bubbles. I'm scrubbing her and she's splashing me.

Coach: You don't want to get soap in anyone's eyes. How about just holding her close while she calms down.

Client: Oh. She put her head on my shoulder. She kicks every once in a while, but she really just loves to be here with me. You know, she's got soft brown hair, kind of thin and fine.

Coach: So ask her what her name is now.

Client: Maria. Her name is Maria.

Coach: So why was she so angry?

Client: She wanted attention and didn't know how else to get it.

Coach: So tell her she doesn't have to get angry to get your attention. She can just talk to you and tell you what she needs.

Client: (to the Inner Child) Maria, you don't have to get angry to get attention. You can just tell me what you want, and I'll be sure to get it for you if I possibly can. You know, I just realized that's like me. I want something sometimes, but don't tell anyone, and then I get angry when they don't read my mind.

Coach: So it sounds like Maria has taken over sometimes when you need something. (client nods) Now what she can do instead is ask you, the Grownup, for what she needs, knowing that your Grownup is fully capable of communicating whatever she needs to anyone.

Client: Yes, I understand. I know I can talk to anyone, provided I'm feeling grown up. It's just when I feel like a little kid that I get scared.

Coach: So the key is to know that those little-kid feelings are in fact the Inner Children's feelings as they look for a caretaker outside yourself. When you have those feelings, get back into your Grownup, speak with the Inner Children to see what they need, and then give it to them—right then and there if you can. Make sure they know that *you* are their caretaker and intend to fulfill that role, no matter what. Tell Maria you know you've let her down many times, and you want her to know you regret that very much. Ask her if she knows that.

Client: Maria, I know I've let you down a lot, and I want you to know I'm very sorry about having done that. I would have taken care of you if I'd known better. I'm really sorry. Do you understand? She says she does.

Coach: Ask her if she'll forgive you for those times.

Client: Can you forgive me for not taking good care of you all those times? She says she's not so sure. She's scared I'm just going to go out and do it again.

Coach: What do you want to say to her?

Client: (Thinks a minute.) Maria, I'd like you to forgive me. It would make it easier for me. But you can take whatever time you need, and I'm going to do my job no matter what. And I'd like you to help me learn what you need by telling me. . . . She says she likes the sound of what I say, but she's going to wait and see.

Coach: That's fine. Tell her you're really glad to be talking with her and that you'd like to give her a gift to play with when you're not talking with her. What would she like?

Client: She says she wants a drawing and paint set.

Coach: How nice! So that's one of the gifts she's bringing to you—a love of artistic expression! Go ahead and give her a set. In fact, how about letting her pick out the set she wants.

Client: I know just the one. It has so many colored pencils—maybe a hundred or so—and special paper and a beautiful wooden box with all the paints in it.

Coach: Pretty fancy.
Client: She's worth it. I really like her.
Coach: Wonderful. Maybe you'd like to do art with her. How about making that one of your promises to her?
Client: Maria, I promise to speak with you at least 3 times a day, and next weekend, we'll spend at least 2 hours with colors and paper making something beautiful.

Sometimes an Inner Child won't answer no matter what you do, and you think you're stalemated. That's not necessarily the case. Often an Inner Child is testing you to see if you'll abandon the process if he or she doesn't perform. Sometimes the Inner Child has decided to resist anything that looks like someone's trying to change him.

Apparent stalemates are often invitations to a healing coach to jump in and take over the Grownup's job of caring for the person. In Inner Family Healing, this is almost never appropriate, especially in later sessions, because it disempowers the person's Grownup and encourages the Inner Children's fantasy that someone outside themselves will finally rescue them and give them what they didn't get when they were little.

In the sessions, we use a variety of different options to deal with stalemate, and noɪe of them involve thinking or acting for the client. Here's what we do: (1) we laugh at our impatience and express our admiration for the Inner Children's determination not to be taken in by anything phony, and then we hang in and simply wait in silence; (2) we call Time Out and break for coffee or tea to discuss what's going on with the person, just as we would with a friend or co-therapist; and/or (3) we talk about our own problems; (4) we may do some rebirthing* to bypass the Inner Children's intellectual resistance and get the energy moving in a nonverbal way so it's available to the Grownup.

None of these options involve thinking or acting for the person's own Grownup. We may give information to the Grownup, but we insist the action come from them. In clinical language, jumping in to care for the Inner Child encourages *transference*. Transference is the term used to describe what happens when an adult person's Inner Child looks to an outsider to satisfy its emotional and physical needs instead of looking to its own Inner

---

* Rebirthing is a gentle form of hyperventilation that helps the body clear energy blocks. See the Bibliography for references.

Grownup. It's crucial that the Inner Children learn that the best caretaking can come only from their own Grownup.

If an Inner Child Is Masquerading as a Grownup

When the Grownup just doesn't seem to be available, it may be that an Inner Child has usurped the Driver's Seat. Here are some exercises for helping the Grownup reclaim control.

1. Change physical position to a more adult stance. If you're sitting, make sure you're not in the teenage slump. Sit up, putting your butt against the back of the chair and make sure your spine is straight. Uncross your arms and legs, and be aware of your whole body.

    Or, you can stand up and feel your full size and strength. Feel your feet on the floor and sense the floor supporting you. Be a tree trunk. Imagine energy pouring through you down into the floor as if your feet have sprouted roots going deep into the earth. Then imagine nutrients and energy being drawn up through your roots through your trunk, and out through your head and shoulders to feed your branches and leaves. Then draw sunlight energy from the leaves back down through the branches and down through your body and then into your root system, and so on.

2. Emulate someone else's Grownup. Pretend you are that person.

3. Envision the healthy Inner Family within you.

4. Call your parents by their first names, in person if you can, and otherwise at least to yourself.

5. Recall situations in which you operated from the Grownup, and recreate the experience of how you felt physically, what you heard, and what you saw.

6. Express feeling to discharge tension. Say "I feel—" followed by whatever you're feeling for as loud and long as you need to.

These exercises can work wonders. Once the Grownup is activated, return to the guidelines for the session.

If the exercises don't work, remember this: An Inner Child who has usurped the position of the Grownup will seldom relinquish its power position without a fight, so resistance is normal. Sometimes one of the Inner Children has established itself as a sort of Guardian-at-the-Gate who allows no change until it's reassured that there's no inherent danger. The Guardian Child may have been startled into action by the simple change in Grownup behavior called for by the promises; however, with information and reassurance, he or she usually begins cooperating with the Grownup's development.

The best thing we've found to do is hang in for a few sessions to educate the person in how the process works and what it can produce. In effect, we work with whichever Inner Family member presents itself on the assumption that, once reassured, the Guardian Child will relinquish its hold on the personality and allow the healing to proceed. Remember, all Inner Children deeply desire a strong, loving Inner Grownup to take care of them, so they are often willing to suspend their power struggle long enough to learn what's possible. Once they catch the vision, they are then willing to relinquish their stranglehold on the person and allow the Grownup to develop.

If you're working on your own, educating yourself would mean reading and rereading this book, and perhaps finding yourself a healing coach to support you and provide encouragement, wisdom, and strength in the discovery process. If even one of the Inner Children is willing to hear about a new way of living, we encourage you to stay with the process to see what the possibilities are.

If the Grownup doesn't become evident in a few sessions, then it's likely the undeveloped Grownup cannot overcome the resistance of all of the Children united against it. In such cases, getting the Inner Grownup into the driver's seat requires outside help and probably a different form of therapy. We discuss this at greater length in the next chapter under "When an Inner Child Sits in the Driver's Seat.

Instructions for Ongoing Inner Family Work

Because each of us is so individual, it's difficult to say much that will apply to everyone. But here are our best answers to some of the questions people ask frequently.

Q: *I can't remember the names of my Inner Children after a while or where they are, or even what they need. Is that a problem?*

We don't think it's a serious problem unless your Inner Kids think it is. Some mind and some don't. You also might try having a good, deep session to find all of them, and then write down what you get: Names, location, ages, gender, favorite things to do, and special gifts and talents. Many are the times we wish we had kept a diary recounting the adventures we've had with our own Inner Children, not only for the purposes of writing this book, but just for the pleasure of seeing how far we've all come together. To give you a sense of the richness such a diary holds, read Appendix B.

Q: *How do I know if I've found all my Inner Children?*

You don't. What you can know is that if addictions aren't running your life, and you have a sense of being an adult in handling difficulties and relationships, those Inner Children who need to be found so far are in fact being cared for. Life itself is therapy and, when the time is right for finding another Inner Child, Life will present a situation that brings that Child within reach.

Q: *I think I'm going to get out of the habit of thinking about the Inner Children if they're not upset or don't seem to need me. What do I do after it feels like I've mainly gotten it together?*

Short answer: Be available to meet new Inner Children, while recognizing at the same time that a good parent does a lot of good parenting automatically, without even having to think about it because of all the practice.

Also, know that undiscovered Inner Children will present themselves when they think you're ready. Here's how we handle that: When we are feeling a persistent upset—when we're particularly angry at someone, for example, or if we notice ourselves being very nervous in a given situation, we assume the feelings are coming from one of the Inner Children. We look for the physical location, we speak to the Child in love as described in Chapter 4. The one who comes up may or may not be one we already know. In the last 6 months, after not having found any for several years, I (Jacqui) have discovered four new Inner Children, Anastasia, Adele, Honey, and Sadie (don't ask me where the names came from).

Q: *What if I'm trying to talk to my kids and they just don't respond at all? I feel kind of silly, but even more important, I don't know if I'm doing it right or if what I'm doing is going to make any difference.*

If you seem not to be reaching the Inner Children, one or more of several things may be happening:

• Your resolve and determination are being tested. The Inner Kids are waiting to see if you'll really keep your word.

• The Inner Children are too young to talk, so you won't hear words; look for feeling instead.

- You have an Inner Child who is stonewalling you. Often this is a teenager, but not necessarily. Look for the location of the sense of resistance or emptiness, and ask what the Child needs.
- You need some assistance in relating to the Inner Children. One reader reported using some old photographs of herself as a child and picturing her Inner Children as looking like them. She found it very helpful. Another possibility is to imagine yourself in a pitch dark room, sitting opposite a silent, hurting Child and simply loving him or her until you can be a light in the darkness for that Inner Child.
- You may need to work with a coach to get the process going.

Whatever you do, don't use an apparent lack of response as an excuse for berating yourself or-deciding that you have so many problems that you're hopeless. That's just more of the same kind of abuse that didn't work when you were growing up.

Q: *Sometimes I just feel depressed and angry or sad for no particular reason and, no matter what I say or do, I can't seem to snap out of it.*

We would like to be able to say that we never feel down, but no one can. Everyone gets depressed from time to time, usually from one of three causes:

1. An impending healing of an old trauma. Sometimes you'll feel depressed when an Inner Child is frightened, sad, and angry about something in his or her past. When it's time for healing that memory, events in the here and now often echo the difficulties of that past situation in some way. You may feel as if you are back at square one, feeling the same old way as if you'd never done any growing or healing. It's not true: As bad as it feels, you're simply about to have another breakthrough. Here's an approach that may move the process along a little faster: First, make sure your Grownup is in the driver's seat by standing up and remembering situations when you acted powerfully. Then, look through and around your body to see where the feelings are focused, put your hand on that place and say to the Inner Child, "I love you and, no matter what happens, I'm never leaving you and I'm never letting you leave me." Then proceed through the steps in chapter 4. The Inner Child you find may be new to you, or it may be a familiar one who is finally revealing a long kept and painful secret.

2. Your neglect or ignorance of some Inner Children's needs. You may feel depressed because you're reverting to old patterns; for

example, you may no longer be speaking with your Inner Children, or you may be allowing one Inner Child to abuse the others, calling them stupid or ugly or mean. When Inner Children begin to feel bad, it's because you've failed to provide enough positive attention, for without positive attention, all clever children will make do with negative attention. Correct the balance of positive and negative by getting your Grownup back in the driver's seat and creating an overflow of genuine appreciation. For more on this, read the next chapter, The Reluctant Grownup.

3. Loss and fatigue. Sometimes what is bothering you isn't from the past at all; it's right here and now. If you've had a loss or disappointment, if you're over-tired, if you've been all-work-and-no-play, if you've been eating poorly, if a large and exciting project has ended and you're not sure what to do with yourself next—any of these and a host of others can produce depression. So use common sense and a few well-tested strategies:

    a. Nurture yourself—with a good book, a hot bath, a massage, some holding from a friend, a walk out in nature, a nap;

    b. Inject fresh interests into your life;

    c. Call a good friend to share your feelings and get support and inspiration;

    d. Get healthy by reducing your sugar intake and exercising aerobically, and

    e. Practice smiling in front of the mirror. (Smiling? You must be kidding!) If you will smile at yourself in the mirror, slowly and broadly fifty times, you will actually change your biochemistry and thus your mood.)

Q: *How long will I have to keep speaking with my Inner Children every day?*

Our experience thus far does not give us a fixed length of time. The best short answer we can give is, As long as it makes a noticeable difference in your life over a couple of week's time. We haven't yet found a time when turning inward and shining a spotlight of besotted affection on our Inner Children fails to make a difference.

Some people find that once a caretaking loop is established, and the Inner Children have learned to trust the Inner Grownup, some or all of the necessary caretaking occurs automatically. Perhaps some of the Inner Children amuse and take care of one another, just as in large families—that seems to be the case at times, but it's important for the

Inner Children to know that's not their job. It's a choice they make freely.

Q: *Do the Inner Children ever grow up or go away?*
    We see no evidence that the Inner Children get any older than they are when we find them. What does happen is they get healed under the influence and safety of your loving attention. They may seem to have "disappeared," because they don't grab the steering wheel so often, but they are still alive and well, and you can generally find them if you choose to.

❖

Not every Grownup chooses to find their Inner Children—in fact, some are quite reluctant, and that is what our next chapter addresses.

6

Empowering the Reluctant Grownup

Since all of us have a Grownup that is underdeveloped in some area of our lives, this chapter pertains to everyone.

It doesn't take long to see that strengthening and re-educating the Grownup is the heart of Inner Family Healing. In fact, healing the Inner Family is impossible unless the Grownup can assume executive control of the person and provide a safe space for the Inner Children to heal. Accordingly, this chapter describes:

1. What it's like to have a powerful Grownup: The vision to aim for
2. What it feels like to have an underdeveloped Grownup
3. What an underdeveloped Grownup looks like from the outside
4. How to strengthen the under-developed Grownup

What It's Like to Have a Powerful Grownup: The Vision to Aim For

When we have a powerful Grownup who consistently cares for our Inner Children in support of our whole person, here's what we experience:

1. *Unconditional love for ourselves.* A Grownup feels compassionate love for the Inner Child personalities no matter what, whether

the Inner Children are happy or blue, angry or frightened, quick or slow.

2. *Safety*. Grownups don't allow Inner Children their own way in all things, but first establish safety through setting and enforcing limits on behavior.

3. *Spontaneity and permission*. When our Grownup has provided true safety to the Inner Children, then our Inner Children have the permission to play and imagine with great freedom, knowing that their Grownup will see to it that they come to no harm. They can also speak freely about what they think, want, and feel, knowing that, if the Grownup has erred, an apology will be forthcoming and forgiveness flow.

4. *Freedom from guilt*. Because the Grownup assumes all responsibility for the Inner Children and their behavior, no matter what, the Inner Children needn't use guilt to control themselves or others. They can make mistakes without beating themselves up. They also are prevented by the Grownup from engaging in activities that would be guilt-producing.

5. *Sharp and sure awareness of the here and now*. When our Grownup is strong and well-established, we know what's going on around us. We can separate feelings and thoughts that belong to the here and now from those that are echoes left over from the past. When those leftover feelings intrude on our perception of the present, we can quickly sort them out and regain accurate awareness in the present.

6. *Confidence*. Being aware of the here and now and having a powerful Grownup gives us confidence and power in both our ability to respond appropriately to what goes on around us and our will to do so. We have self-discipline; that is, we know we can handle Inner Child impulses internally in the interests of taking care of our greatest long-term good. As a result, we can count on ourselves to do what we say we will.

For those of us from dysfunctional families, these experiences are either intermittent or alien. Many of us don't even know what Grownup functioning looks like, because we were raised by parents whose Inner Children occupied the driver's seat most of the time.

As a result, for most of us, once we discover our Inner Children, it's typical to discover at the same time our Grownup hasn't been running our lives any more than our parents' Grownups ran theirs. What we find instead is that our lives have been run by very clever, controlling Inner Children who are masquerading as adults. The following should sound familiar.

What It Feels Like When the Grownup Is Underdeveloped

A common experience of people who lack a developed Grownup is best described by Anne, in speaking of her first 40 years.

Dear Mary,

You've asked me to describe what it was like before I had any substantial Grownup functioning. As I look back on my life, much of what I see looks like something that had more to do with someone else than with me. That's how far I've come. Thank goodness for hindsight—it's helped me make sense out of what made very little sense at the time—and to have hope when I get discouraged. If I could get to here from where I started, I can do anything!

To keep from writing all day, I'm going to cover just a few topics: conformity; fear and other feelings; intuition; sexuality; and feeling like a kid in an adult world.

Conformity. When I was in my twenties, I considered myself independent. What is painfully evident now is I was anything but. The truth was, I felt OK only as long as I was doing what I thought my mother and father would approve of or not care about. As soon as I began stretching the edges of what they would have considered acceptable behavior or making my own decisions and being successful at it, I became visibly nervous—to others. I myself wasn't even aware of being fearful. It took a friend saying, "Hey Anne, I've never seen you like this. You're like a cat on a hot tin roof." I wasn't even sure what he was talking about at the time, but I remember it all these years later. Now I realize I was just a scared kid, trying to behave like a Grownup.

Fear and other feelings. That incident highlighted another feature of my experience as an adult with an inadequate Grownup functioning. Despite my nervous behavior, in those days, I had no conscious experience of fear, except when my car skidded on the ice or something.

It wasn't until my thirties, when I began to meditate, that I was able to slow down and feel my feelings. At that point, I started realizing I was scared most of the time. I could avoid it with work (for years a reliable refuge where I could shine), I could find myself a protector, or I could fake my way out of it—if I acted like my mother—bright and chirpy, always in a hurry, interested in everything, or having a temper tantrum. But these defense mechanisms were devices of a frightened Inner Child, not a Grownup woman. And they only worked partially. They could never overcome this persistent sense that living fully wasn't safe. I always needed to keep myself in check for fear of doing something wrong. Every time I reached out to do something, it seemed there was an almost equal force saying—careful there, not too much, watch out—for what, I never knew.

Intuition. One of the reasons I was so frightened was that my Inner Child had long ago decided to reduce the confusion in her life by blocking out intuitive perception. The things people said in my family were a lot nicer than what they did, so I decided I would block out any awareness of what they did and see what I could do to make what they said come true—in my imagination if nowhere else. I don't remember when I cut off my intuition—but I do remember getting into one kind of pickle after another because I'd listen to what people said, but ignore what they actually did. Doing that meant I didn't have to deal with the fact that their words and actions didn't match. When I couldn't avoid that incongruity, I would think obsessively, in a panic, trying desperately to make a coherent picture out of it all that didn't make anyone wrong, except maybe me. Without intuition to guide me, I felt very vulnerable, and I didn't trust myself or anyone else.

Feeling like a kid. I don't know if this was related or not, but I also felt as if others were adults, but I was just a kid. I acted like a kid. For example, if someone began to question me closely on something, I'd first be reasonable and placating, then angry and defensive, and then I'd start looking for the door. I'm reminded of the movie, *Big,* which told the story of a little boy who wished to be a big man, and was granted his wish. He was about 10 years old, and it was tough for him. A lot of the time, I was a lot younger than he was.

Sexuality. The sense of being a child was especially pronounced around people who were very assured sexually. The men I chose were equally insecure and childlike in their own way. It never occurred to me that a real man would have chosen someone like me. I'll never know, because I vanished before any of them could get that close. As for having children or doing any of those other adult things, I felt totally unequipped. I didn't even feel fully female, as if my sexuality had somehow gotten lost between being little and getting as big as I was. I certainly looked female enough, and I didn't have any inclination to be male, but sexuality was like unknown territory.

So that's what it felt like to have a nonfunctioning Grownup. Just writing this makes me appreciate how far I've come. Thanks for your help on the journey. I love you two.

Examples of What the Underdeveloped Grownup Looks Like From the Outside

From an outsider's standpoint, it's clear that people need to strengthen the Grownup when they:

1. Fail to look after their own well-being
2. Manipulate others into looking after them
3. Rebel continually against authority overtly or covertly
4. Lapse into any of these patterns in specific areas.

Here are some more examples of people whose Grownups have been underdeveloped. Perhaps you'll recognize some of them.

Failing to Look After One's Own Well-Being

ARTIE was not a client of ours, but someone we observed in a hospital setting as a perfect example of someone with an undeveloped Grownup. A World War II veteran, Artie had been a happy-go-lucky man, married with three kids. He had worked hard as a barman at Schrafft's and at another place to earn extra money for his family. He had been known for being helpful and kind to all his customers. When we met him forty years later in the hospital, he was divorced, alcoholic, and very ill. His legs were the color of blue plums because of poor circulation. Periodically he became so ill that he had to go back to the hospital. The hospital was his second home.

One visit, he was told that his legs would have to be amputated due to gangrene if he didn't get treatment immediately. However, he couldn't drink while the treatment was being given.

Although he knew the risk, he continued to drink and his Inner Children, one especially, saw his benefactors at the hospital as opponents in a contest in which their aim was to trap him into a treatment program, and his was to escape their trying to spoil his fun. So Artie's Inner Children continued to play Catch-me-if-you-can, not realizing that he would be caught regardless, either by the alcohol or the gangrene, and there would be no escape. Indeed there wasn't, for Artie lost his legs and is now in rehab learning to live with his disability. Undaunted, his Inner Child hasn't yet given up the game, and he looks forward to having a few drinks with his buddies when he's free of the rehab.

Manipulating Others into Caretaking

FRANCES, 55, 150 pounds overweight, brilliant, was waited on hand and foot in her childhood by her mother, father, and grandmother. Love in her family was expressed by urging to eat the best of good food.

Later in life, Frances, if invited to a party, fully expected her host to be responsible for picking her up and taking her home and demanded to be waited on, albeit with gentle voice, sweet smile, and an expression of appealing helplessness. So painful was it for more agile bodies to see her heave herself up out of her chair and stagger toward getting anything for herself that they leapt to her assistance. Frances also expected the choicest morsels of food, which she asked for with the wide-eyed look look of an 18-month-old who, having been good, now looks for her reward. Appealing in a baby, in an adult her pleas were repulsive.

We're pleased to write that Frances, in the process of claiming her own power to care for her own appetites today, is down 100 pounds and has completely revised the way she prefers to eat. She is no longer helpless and self-focused; rather she is moving more and more into a giving mode, contributing to the well-being of others in the process.

Rebelling Against Authority

ANGELA is a chic career woman in her sixties. She lives on her own with a small Skye terrier named Pixie, whom she adores. Angela was living in an apartment building that was slated to go condo. She had been warned by her landlord that if she didn't prevent Pixie from depositing little balls of dog poop on the way into the entrance hall, he would take action.

Angela was peppered with warnings, verbal and written. She ignored them all. The landlord, who knew he could clear $40,000 on her apartment if he could evict her, amassed a file evidencing Angela's rebellious behavior as an undesirable.

When the case came to court, Angela was evicted. Her loss on the value of the apartment over the next 3 years exceeded $100,000, which would have come in very handy as retirement time rolls around.

When we confronted her with her behavior in this instance, Angela finally saw that if she failed to develop her Grownup, she would likely repeat the pattern. It gives us great joy to be able to write that Angela has a wonderful Grownup who is doing an excellent job of caring for her Inner Children. Pixie is also behaving beautifully, while Angela wields the pooper scooper in the manner born.

JOHN, 45, a brilliant therapist with an MSW degree, has had a speckled career. He has been a therapist in a residential treatment center for drug addicts, promoter for a rock band, a disk jockey, and currently, a state trooper. He also had a record of arrests that stretches from Oregon to Louisiana.

Addicted to many things, narcotics among them, John sees the world with the starkness of a cynic and gets his kicks chiefly from beating the system. His greatest coup and source of delight was being able to con the state troopers into accepting him on the force.

John has "gone straight" a number of times. The problem is that when he does so, he considers himself a sucker. Therefore, while he knows right from wrong, he chooses to follow the way of the con man. One Inner Child, who decided that he would beat the authorities before the authorities could beat him, runs his life. For that Child, the prospect of giving up what he has defined as the winning position on his filmstrip carries with it all the emotional impact of death. Sadly, in insisting on living his way, he is killing the man that John could have been.

The foregoing examples represent people whose Inner Children have usurped the Grownup's role almost completely, forcing the person to depend on others and to forfeit the power needed to fulfill their potential.

The next two examples illustrate what happens when the Grownup is in the driver's seat most of the time, but loses control to one or more of the Inner Children in certain situations.

Lapsing in Specific Areas

The following two examples illustrate how someone's Grownup can be operating well, even superbly in some areas and virtually not at all in others.

EDWIN is a man who pulled himself out of a background of deep poverty to become a highly successful, sophisticated executive and philanthropist. Everything he has done in the outer world has been brilliant, characterized by the unusual thinking style that helped him achieve such success.

No such brilliance has characterized his relationships with women, however. Although the women in his life have all been beautiful, talented, and entirely eligible as life partners, he has stopped short of becoming involved on a permanent basis. His opinion that marriage is not a viable arrangement camouflages a profound terror of being controlled. As soon as a woman wants a permanent commitment, he terminates the relationship. In fact, he's even ambivalent toward sex, for he sees his need for it as the one thing that makes him vulnerable to women's domination, women's will.

Conditioned by the fiercely ambitious mother who demanded success above all from her offspring to bolster her own self worth, his Inner Child sees all women as relentless, demanding, and domineering persecutors. One Inner Child is enraged, while another, younger, desperately longs for the kind of unconditional acceptance that he should have had.

We are happy to report that as of this writing, Edwin has committed to a full experience of learning to care for himself. As long as we still have our sanity, it's never too late.

HELGA is a superb teacher, independent in her thinking, meticulous in her preparation, capable of creating in her classroom an atmosphere of such safety that children progress at speeds well beyond what the system says is possible. She is married, very contentedly, to an attractive, able, amusing man with whom she shares many interests. They have two children. Helga's thinking and organizational abilities enable her to manage her job, her house, her children, and a modestly active social life, all the while maintaining an excellent sense of humor.

However, she has a pattern of running into colleagues who both compete with her and exploit her. They pick her brains, entice her to volunteer with them for special projects, let her do all the work, and then run away with accolades that she and she alone has truly earned. She feels used and abused, angry, frightened of saying anything, and confused. From being a fully competent teacher, she seems to become a terrified, whining child, looking in vain for someone else to fight her battles for her.

What Helga is reacting to is her Family Spell. Her Family Spell filmstrip includes a sister on whom her manic-depressive mother bestowed all her affection, meanwhile abusing Helga severely, physically, sexually and emotionally, demanding that Helga play the role of Cinderella. So when someone at work, especially a female, competes with her, Helga sees her as her sister and immediately looks for her mother—an authority figure to take sides against her. She may also find a person to play her father, a gentle man with a good heart who nevertheless turned a blind eye to the mental and physical abuse that his wife heaped on Helga.

How does a functioning Grownup gets thrown out of the driver's seat? it's usually because a scene on the filmstrip has been activated that an Inner Child considers a threat to survival. When the scene is activated, the Inner Child overwhelms the body—and thereby the Grownup—with a biochemical flood we know as fear or rage or guilt. When more than one Inner Child is affected, with one Inner Child signaling fear (run) and one signaling rage (fight), the result is paralysis or a feeling of being crazy.

Basic Strategy for Strengthening the Grownup

How you go about strengthening the Grownup over the longer term depends on which of two situations applies:

1. The Grownup is in the Driver's seat and functioning most of the time, (as with Helga and Edwin), but lacks important knowledge and skills in certain areas and periodically gets thrown off balance by a terrified Inner Child.
2. The one in the Driver's seat is actually an Inner Child, possibly masquerading as a Grownup, possibly in outright rebellion.

When the Grownup is the executive most of the time, shifting one's behavior is relatively easy. Skills acquired in one part of life are usually transferrable. Helga, for example, could use her fine skills in the classroom to reassure and encourage her Inner Children and to discipline her own behavior. Edwin, should he choose to do so, can use his professional and business persistence to analyze his behavior and identify which Inner Children have such hatred and fear of women.

Where the Children are in the Driver's seat most of the time, strengthening the Grownup is a more complicated process, for a Grownup may not even be evident, much less capable of wresting executive control from the Inner Children.

We'll take a look at strategies for dealing with both these situations, including guidelines for knowing when and how to get help.

When the Grownup Is Already in the Driver's Seat

There are six main parts to the strategy for strengthening an already functioning Grownup.

1. Use physical posture to elicit grownup behavior.
2. Exercise the ability to make and keep commitments, starting with very small things and then moving on to larger ones.
3. Learn the power of genuine apology and restitution for broken commitments.
4. Educate Grownup in identifying and interrupting harmful patterns.
   a. Explain the theory of the Family Spell.
   b. Define Games (specific present-day problem behaviors) and show how they recreate pictures from the Family Spell filmstrip both internally and externally.
   c. Explain how to use Karpman's drama triangle.
5. Commit to clear, open communication.
6. Use encouragement to reinforce Grownup behavior. We'll discuss each of these in turn.

Use Physical Posture to Elicit Grownup Behavior

Did you know you can actually cheer yourself up by smiling, even if you feel sad? Smiling releases chemicals into the bloodstream that relieve depression. And this is only one instance of how, in a deliberate, conscious "fake-it-till-you-make-it" way, you can call forth that which you choose to emulate. Body posture not only communicates information to others, it also communicates that same information to ourselves.

The mechanism that works for smiling and feeling happy works just as well in empowering the Grownup. In fact, we can and do use it to put any Inner Family member in executive control.

As an experiment, use your body to be a scared little kid. Sit on the floor, cross-legged, slump your shoulders, trying to make yourself small, and bend your neck so your head is to the side and you're looking up. Stop breathing for a little bit, and then after a little while, make your breathing very shallow.

Now be a rebellious teenager: Slide down in a chair, stick your legs out, fold your arms, assume a sullen you-can't-make-me facial expression, and realize that in order to make you do what you don't want to do (which is just about anything), they'll probably have to lose their cool. You win either way. You can achieve the same effect standing up. Stand, with your feet about shoulder width apart and your weight on one hip, lock your knees, cave in your chest, fold your arms, and stick out your stomach.

Now move from the rebellious stance into being a Grownup. Here's how you do it so you're truly a Grownup and not a kid masquerading as a Grownup according to early parental patterns.

1. *Shift so you are evenly balanced on both feet and rock back so your weight is on your heels.* When you feel as if you're about to tip over backwards, bend your knees slightly and unlock your pelvis so it's easy to move.

2. *Expand your breathing.* First, to relax and widen your shoulders and back, swing your arms forward, up, back, and around. Let your shoulders and chest expand. Breathe with your back as well as your chest.

3. *Imagine that your spine is hanging like a rope* straight down from under the back of your skull. To do this, those of us who are swaybacked have to make a conscious effort to tuck our tail-bones in.

4. *Imagine your skull is floating* about an inch or two above the very top of the spine, so that there is enough airspace for someone to pass a finger between the spine and the skull. This lengthens your spine and eases tension in your neck.

5. *Let your chin drop* until a straight line drawn from your forehead to your chin would be perpendicular to the floor.

6. *Begin grounding yourself with an energy meditation.* Imagine that you are a tree trunk, and that roots are extending from your toes deep into the earth. Feel them take in moisture and nutrients from the earth and send them up through your body to the

branches, which are growing out of your head and shoulders. Then, take in the sunlight and warmth and send it down again through your body and feet to nourish and strengthen your root system. Notice that you are in charge of this energy, that you can choose to receive it or refuse it. You have this energy always with you, because you are always connected to the earth. Notice how it empowers and nourishes the whole person, including all your Inner Children.

Exercise the Ability to Make and Keep Appropriate Commitments

Making and keeping appropriate commitments to the Inner Children is the number one priority in Inner Family Healing. If you are able to do nothing else, that will be enough. Like most simple things, however, it's easier said than done. Here are some guidelines:

1. Visualize successes ahead of time.
2. Start small, to build the habit of winning, and be sure to cover these items: communication, loving care, appreciation, and protection, e.g.,

    — I will speak with you, my Inner Child, for two minutes once a day for a week
    — I will buy one toy for one Inner Child this week
    — I will take 90 seconds three times a day to check in with all my Inner Children, to tell each one I love them, and to hear what they need
    — I will get a professional massage once in the next 10 days
    — I will write down two things I appreciate about each of my Inner Children
    — I promise to say no to the next 3 tasks that my grown biological children ask me to do that they can do themselves and spend the time on my own leisure instead
    — I promise to leave the next situation where someone is trying to intimidate me.
3. Get support from a friend, someone to cheer you on.

Learn About Apology and Restitution

We inevitably fail in keeping our promises. Even after the Grownup is fully established, we let ourselves and our Inner Children down. When that happens, some of us tend to blame the Inner Children. We may say, for example, "They knew and I didn't," or, "If they weren't so troublesome, I would have been able to do the job" and similar excuses. As attractive as this argument may seem to the Grownup, it's not the truth and therefore can't solve anything. The Grownup is *always* responsible, not for what others do, but what we do, for what we allow the Inner Children to do.

When you've broken a commitment, to protect, to communicate, to love, and to appreciate, here's how to apologize and make restitution for it:

1. Confess immediately to the Inner Children what you did.
2. Say you regret having done it.
3. Ask the Inner Child, "Will you forgive me?"
4. Say to the Inner Child, I'd like to make up for it, and
   a. Here's what I'll do, or
   b. What can I do that would help make up for it?
5. Give Inner Children time to discharge bad feelings and forgive you when they feel like it.

In the beginning, taking responsibility can be difficult for the Grownup for three reasons. First, although we know we're bound to to make mistakes, simply because we don't know everything, we see mistakes as failure. Failure hurts our pride and makes us feel like we're being made wrong for not being God-like. The truth is that Grownups, fallible as they are, still know more about what's appropriate than any of their Inner Children. Furthermore, no one else is available to take responsibility.

Second, we confuse responsibility with blame. Blaming someone means labeling them bad or wrong or stupid and, often, punishing them. In the healthy Inner Family, although there are consequences, there is no blame.

Third, we don't know how to forgive ourselves, so we project our sense of shame onto our Inner Children. Reading Chapter 9 - "Forgiveness - An Act of Self-Esteem" should clear this up.

Going through the apology and restitution process becomes easier after one has gotten used to it, because the Grownup begins to appreciate that true repentance and forgiveness enables one to start fresh, makes mistakes safe, and engenders trust between the Grownup and the Inner Children.

Teach the Grownup to Identify and Interrupt Harmful Games

Everybody, without exception, plays Games. Playing Games is a major mechanism by which we recreate in our current lives the one-up, one-down relationships of our Family Spell. They are also a powerful vehicle for obtaining strokes and attention without risking the exposure involved in true intimacy.

Game theory was first developed by the late Eric Berne, father of Transactional Analysis and author of *Games People Play*. We're going to present his theories as well as those of Steven Karpman who added his brilliant Drama Triangle as a way to analyze Games.

A Game can be defined as "a series of unconsciously-motivated exchanges between two people that ends in one or both players feeling bad about self, other, and/or the world." You've been in a Game if you find yourself asking two questions:

- Why does this always happen to me?
- How did I get myself into this kind of situation again!?"

Eric Berne catalogued many different Games, *"Stupid," "NIGYSOB* (Now I've Got You, You SOB)," *"Ain't It Awful," "Let's You and Him Fight,"* but the following story of Andy and Vera will serve to illustrate the most important elements common to all Games.

> Andy was a minister, dedicated, very hardworking, with a great desire to be of true service. One day, one of his parishioners, Vera, stopped him after church and said, "Oh Reverend, I am having such troubles. Can you help me?" Andy, full of zeal, replied "Of course. I'd be happy to help." Thus began a series of meetings in which Vera poured out her troubles to him, and he responded with sympathy and helpful advice. It became apparent, however, after a few months of this, that Vera's troubles weren't yielding at all: Nothing was changing. Andy urged her more strongly to put some of his recommendations into practice, but for each recommendation, Vera had a reason why it couldn't work for her.
>
> Finally one day, exasperated with the process, Andy snapped, "Well, if you'd actually do some of the things I've been suggesting instead of just moaning about your life, Vera, I'd feel a lot better about counseling with you." Startled, Vera burst into tears and then jumped to her feet, crying, "I thought you were different, but you're just like all the rest of the ministers. You think you know

everything, and you don't have any idea. Try walking in my shoes and then see if you can stand yourself!" She then rushed out of the office, feeling misunderstood, desperate, and angry at herself for trusting a man, especially a minister, and leaving Andy feeling guilty, angry, and wondering how things turned out so badly—again.

Andy and Vera's vignette illustrates a very common Game called *"Why don't you—yes, But,"* in which one person seeks attention using the ploy Please-help-me (but-you-can't-make-me-change); the other person, needing to be useful, responds with Let-me-help-you (you-need-fixing), but to no avail. The two parties separate having exchanged some strokes, but risked no true intimacy or basic change in their lives.

To keep out of Games, one of the first commandments is learn to recognize when you've gotten into a Game in the first place. (This isn't always easy, for Games, by definition, are played by the Inner Children without the Grownup's conscious awareness. If you know you're playing a Game, you aren't—what you're doing is something else.) For learning to recognize Game patterns, we've never found a more useful device than Steven Karpman's Drama Triangle. The Drama Triangle is used to describe in an uncomplicated way how people move through the different one-up and one-down positions involved in Games. Here's what it looks like:

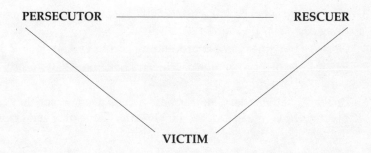

PERSECUTOR ——————————— RESCUER

VICTIM

The three positions, Persecutor and Rescuer (one-up) and Victim (one-down), each have their associated attitudes and feelings. In our example, Vera began as Victim (of her troubles, feeling sad and frightened, needing someone to help, except she doesn't define how) to Andy's Rescuer (of course I can help you, even if I don't know what you want, feeling proud and happy that he is strong enough to help someone). Then, when Andy got angry about Vera not acting on his advice, he switched positions to

Persecutor, where he felt impatient, disapproving, and angry. Then Vera switched, competing for Persecutor (you men/ministers are all alike! and feeling wounded and angry) and thus driving him to the Victim position (What did I do wrong? How did I get myself into this fix again? Parishioners are never satisfied" and feeling weak, frightened, hurt, and resentful). Neither party is ungenuine in their thoughts and feelings; they simply don't realize they've been in a Game.

None of the three positions is a Grownup position. They are occupied and played out only by Inner Children. So once one has become aware that a Game is or has been occurring, the next step is to move to the Grownup, to get the Grownup into the driver's seat. This may be easier said than done, as we've noted before, but we assure you if you are determined, you can do it.

Here's the basic strategy:

1. If you're in the middle of a Game, call for time out. Leave if you must, but don't allow the Inner Children to take it further.

2. Don't take the payoff of bad feeling at the end of the Game. If the end of the Game is feeling miserable or self-righteous, do whatever you have to in order to keep from indulging yourself in the feeling. Breathe deeply, drink a lot of water, do some exercise to clear the body of the emotions' biochemical elements.

3. Replace the usual payoff with something else, preferably something distinctly pleasurable.

4. Observe how the Game is proceeding and how it starts.

5. Focus in on one's own Inner Children's behaviors, not the other person's behavior.

6. Realize that the Inner Children have a deep need, which they're playing the Game in order to satisfy—the Game may even look to them like a matter of life and death.

7. Identify and meet that need in another way. Say to the Inner Children,
    *   I love you.
    *   You may have made the best choices back then, and I thank you for that.
    *   Today those choices are no longer appropriate: You're trying to get others to give you what you didn't get enough of back then. But you can't change the past; and today, the only

person from whom you can really get what you need is me, the Grownup. No one else can do that for you.

- I, the Grownup, can give you what you need today, and I will learn to do that very well.

Here's another useful and important key to understanding Games: Although Games look like they're played mainly on the outside, between one human being and another, those outer games are only a symptom of a more deeply embedded internal process going on between two or more of the Inner Children. That process is powered by the Inner Children's long-ago decision to take care of themselves in the best way they know how in the absence of a caring, protective, available adult.

As with external Games, the Karpman triangle applies. You can find the Inner Child who plays Victim, the Inner Child who plays Persecutor, and even an Inner Child who Rescues. Each plans a role to meet a need that, today, the Grownup can meet in healthier ways. When the Grownup meets those needs and thus frees the Inner Children from the need to play the internal Game, they stop controlling the external behavior.

Much more is written on Games than we're going to include here, but one book is invaluable for stopping Games played by those of us who prefer the Victim position: It's called *Sweet Suffering: Woman as Victim*, by Natalie Shainness. We regret the title—plenty of men suffer and invite suffering without knowing what they're doing or why, and so this is a book for everyone. Chapter 4 contains priceless information on how Victims signal their willingness to be victimized.

Commit to Clear, Open Communication

One of the most effective ways to empower the Grownup is to speak out even in the face of confusion, abuse, conflicting signals, or broken agreements, rather than keeping silent.

Speaking our truth honors it. And when we honor our own truth in the spoken word, when our Grownup sends a clear and potent message that we expect others to do likewise, we reserve for *ourselves* the right to approve or disapprove of ourselves, to reject or accept ourselves. We don't abdicate that right to others.

In some situations, of course, it's only common sense to withhold the truth about the way we think and feel, and even about how we behave, but we're not talking about those situations here. What we're talking about is the kind of enslaving situation in which we hand over power to another person or persons or institution, and in so doing, rob ourselves of two things: (1) validation of our own thoughts and feelings; and (2) the right to choose what we do about them and what happens around us.

What is the right time to speak our truth? as soon as we know what it is *and* can speak it from our Grownup. Inner Children tend toward blaming, either themselves or others, because: (1) they don't always realize they are the source of their own feelings, and (2) they've learned behavior patterns very early in life, before they've developed the perspective to make an adult decision about whether they actually want to do those things or not. The educated Grownup can allow the Inner Children to have their feelings safely, and then choose how to deal with the situation to take care of the whole person.

One of the benefits of speaking one's truth early in the game is that by doing so, one often short circuits a Game. Often uncomfortable feelings signal that a Game is beginning, and speaking out in a straight way interrupts the covert communication that characterize the opening transactions of a Game.

Since Games are such a powerful and predictable source of negative strokes, it's important to make sure we replace those negative strokes with others that are positive. It's long been understood that without strokes, babies die, and that negative strokes are far, far better than none at all. So if we don't fill our cup from another source, we are sure to go back to the source we know best. That's why reward systems are so important.

Use Encouragement to Reinforce Grownup Behavior

If the secret to driving successfully down the road of life is having a loving powerful Grownup in the driver's seat, then the key that starts the engine is encouragement. Without reinforcement and encouragement, not one of us makes much of a Grownup, so encouraging and creating pleasurable rewards for the Grownup is absolutely crucial.

One of the best pleasures is sharing the journey with someone else. So do invite a friend, sponsor, or therapist with whom to share your Inner Family work—a friend, a pastor or rabbi, a therapy group, or a local support group, such as a 12-step or church group—any gathering of people who are consciously growing. You will invariably find support and encouragement there.

To further encourage yourself, we also recommend you:
1. *Make a Delight List:* List what delights and strengthens you in your life
2. *Document wins;* that is, write down every time you experience

a win (meaning you have truly exercised your Grownup authority and responsibilities in new ways for you)

3. *Reward yourself* from the Delight List every time you write down a win.

Encouragement is such an important part of healing the Inner Family that it makes sense to learn a little more about it.

What Encouragement Is And Why It's So Important

Why is encouragement so important? First and foremost because it strengthens the Grownup in staying in the driver's seat, taking care of the Inner Children, while navigating through the changes that make up our lives. If Inner Children don't trust their Grownup, they usually react to change by grabbing the steering wheel again, trying to reestablish control. Even if they do trust the Grownup, sometimes they just can't help themselves, and they grab the steering wheel anyway, even if they would prefer not to.

When the Grownup is encouraged and encouraging, the Inner Children develop the confidence needed to leave the driving to us. Encouragement provides a positive energy source for the whole person, and a fantastic one. Just take a look at these definitions taken from several different dictionaries.

Courage, from the Latin cor, meaning heart, is defined as "the attitude or response of facing and dealing with anything recognized as dangerous, difficult, or painful, instead of withdrawing from it; the quality of being fearless or brave; valor; pluck." Other synonyms for courage include:

Bravery	Enterprise	Gallantry	Mettle
Boldness	Fearlessness	Hardihood	Pluck
Daring	Firmness	Heroism	Resolution
Dauntlessness	Fortitude	Intrepidity	Valor

If we say no more than "give courage to," we say a great deal. But encouragement means even more . . .

Aid	Embolden	Inspirit (to infuse	Promote
Advance	Favor	spirit, life into;	Reassure
Abet	Foster	to enliven self)	Restore
Animate	Forward	Inspire with	confidence
Assure	Give courage to	spirit, courage,	Second
Cheer	Hearten	or strength of mind	Support
Comfort	Help	Instigate	Urge
Countenance	Impel		

These words are a feast for the heart, and if you're open to them being available to you, simply reading them can make a difference in how you feel.

Putting Encouragement in Your Life

We urge you to think purposefully about increasing the flow of encouragement in two contexts: The first context is daily life. Externally, you receive encouragement given to you by others; internally, your Inner Co-therapist encourages your Grownup who passes it on to the Inner Children. The second context is crisis, and the source is spiritual, for those times where you simply don't have in you what you need in order to cope. At those times, Divine encouragement is accessed through a special kind of surrender.

Everyday Encouragement. To get encouragement into our everyday lives, externally and internally, we need first to ask for encouragement from others, and then develop the habit of encouraging ourselves. Here's an example of one person doing both:

> I was in a group, struggling against my addiction to taking care of other people whether they liked it or not, and I asked the group to help me free myself of this addiction. So strong was my Inner Child's tendency to rescue, that I had to write out how I wanted them to help me, because otherwise, she would have sabotaged my Grownup's speaking out.
>
> While still standing there after reading my request, I congratulated myself by squeezing my shoulder and telling myself (out loud) how brave I had just been. I can still recall the delight my Inner Child felt when I did that. . . .

One of the things that you notice, and that will strengthen your own self-talk, is how you begin encouraging others. Doing so is an expression of generosity and optimism, of belief in a person's inherent ability to grow and learn.

Encouraging others in this way is also one of the antidotes to a syndrome that sometimes slows us down. Listen as this same person goes on to describe not only the positive results, but some of what we may all run into from time to time. . .

> . . . However, at the same time my Inner Child was delighted, I could sense the resistance of the group, a subtle disapproval of my pleasure.

In retrospect, I can see that I was challenging the status quo, and giving myself a pat on the back for doing so, while they were nervously trying to figure out how to make me predictable again so they would know how to behave around me.

The question I faced was, would I suppress and starve myself to take care of others' fear of my changing? or would I put my own Inner Children's safety and well-being first, strike out on my own, and sit down to enjoy the feast that is freely available to me? There was no contest, once I realized that the group couldn't actually give me the love I was looking for anyway.

As this example shows, giving yourself encouragement to operate beyond your well-established behavioral boundaries may elicit resistance, not only from one or more of your Inner Children, but also from some of the people nearest to you. Their responses suggest to us that it's OK to change around the fringes, but real change, true freedom, threatens predictability, and therefore control. Ultimately and repeatedly, we all come to such crossroads, and freedom may look like it costs us everything we hold dear.

As you find yourself facing those kinds of resistance, there are two things to remember: First, those who fear your changes can learn—they can learn that you don't leave, or stop loving them, or hurt them. They can learn that your being a free and courageous person can be a blessing to them. They can learn to join you! And you can learn that it's OK for people to adjust to you, instead of you being the one to accommodate to them.

The second thing to remember is that others can share in your victories as you express your gratitude for the contributions they've made to your freedom. Because they *have* contributed: those close to us, in some way or another, have made some kind of direct or indirect contribution, whether we liked it at the time or not. By acknowledging those contributions, and showing appropriate gratitude for them, we safeguard ourselves from the hazards of thinking that we did it all by ourselves, which merely feeds our Inner Children's most grandiose fantasies. As long as we know we're only making it because of the additional support that comes to us, we keep our power and that of others in perspective.

Divine Encouragement. There are times when, as much as we would like to love our Inner Children and as much as we would like to have courage, we lack love, strength, and courage, and nothing anyone else can say fills the gap. At such times we're forced to accept our own limitations and to call on other resources. Just as there are no atheists in foxholes, so, when our last ounce of will and strength has been exhausted, we turn to another Source.

I can say in all honesty that there were times in the last 10 years of looking after my mother and her Alzheimer's, I have had no strength even to call for encouragement, much less give it to myself. At those times, my strength has come from partaking of Communion daily for the last 7 years, and from answers to prayer.

Looking at the lists defining courage and encouragement, I can truly say that what I receive in answer to prayer is encouragement. When I find myself struggling to wash my mother in the shower, and she, with all the strength of her Welsh peasant background, is fighting me, I call upon God and it works. Even if I have to shout the Hail Mary with my teeth clenched and wanting to kill, something happens, and I am able to complete my task. What I get may be strength to move her, it may be patience to wait till she relaxes (or, more likely, tires herself out), or it may be humor, to soothe and relax my own soul. Whatever it is, I accept it as encouragement, and I become more than I thought I could be.

When an Inner Child Sits in the Driver's Seat

We hear people say, "I don't *have* a Grownup!" When that or a similar statement is made consistently over a period of time, we've learned that an Inner Child who has taken primary responsibility for the person's survival is firmly ensconced in the Driver's seat with no other Inner Children inclined to challenge him or her. We describe that Inner Child as having executive control. The person can't experience the Grownup because this Inner Child won't allow it for fear of losing control over the ability to survive.

When an Inner Child controls the personality, healing the Inner Family means completely restructuring internal relationships. This can be quite a job, principally because the person whose Inner Child is in control generally identifies with that Inner Child and may have little or no awareness of the Grownup's existence.

The person needn't create a Grownup where none existed before; a Grownup exists whether it is in evidence or not. However, the restructuring often requires long periods of retraining and developing the Grownup's parenting muscles and further periods of wrestling with Inner Children who can't easily give up the power they've been exercising for so long.

Healing and reorganizing an Inner Family that is being run by an executive Inner Child is close to impossible without a healing coach. It takes time and help from others to learn to distinguish between the Grownup and the pseudo-Grownup, the masquerading Child.

Even with a coach, the restructuring is possible only if the Inner Children are willing to allow access to the Grownup. In some cases, the person may want relief from pain, but one or more Inner Children remain adamant about running the person's existence (like John, above, who beats the system no matter what the cost). If all the Inner Children gang up against the Grownup, the Grownup can't win and everybody loses.

When we can't access the Grownup fairly consistently after four or five sessions, then instead of or in addition to Inner Family healing, we recommend other modalities.

1. An emotionally-based therapy like bioenergetics, New Identity Process (the Casriel method), or rebirthing can help a person learn to navigate through their own emotional landscape and release stored-up feelings from the past.

2. Other therapies invite a client into a transferential relationship, in which the therapist becomes something of a substitute parent with whom a person can work out unresolved trust issues. These include transactional analysis combined with gestalt, psychoanalysis, rational-emotive therapy.

3. Going to a therapist isn't the only way: If substance abuse or other types of addiction are involved, 12-step groups such as Alcoholics Anonymous (AA), Alanon, Narcotics/Gamblers/ Codependents Anonymous (NA,GA,CODA), and Adult Children of Alcoholics (ACOA) may provide an opening for deeper work.

4. If those therapeutic modalities don't work, it's comforting to know that life itself is therapy, and it offers each one of us repeated invitations to grow.

Our strategy is to work with and educate whatever members of the person's Inner Family are available until we're clear that: (1) Inner Family Healing can really work for them, with or without a coach; (2) Inner Family Healing is premature and another type of therapy is indicated; or (3) Inner Family Healing needs to be augmented with another type of therapy.

In reaching those conclusions, we follow these basic steps.

1. We make an agreement with the Inner Children to accept the existence of the Inner Family as a working hypothesis.

2. We enlist the aid of what we call the Inner Observer, which is the part of the Grownup that does not do caretaking *per se*. This part simply watches and takes note of what goes on.

3. We teach about permissions and limits.

4. We teach the person to catch the Grownup in action and document it: That means gathering evidence in sessions, asking friends and perhaps business associates what they see of Grownup functioning, and writing it down for reference and reinforcement.

5. We acknowledge and praise the Grownup for effective behavior.

If you are working alone, then you would parallel these steps as follows:

1. Accept the existence of the Inner Family as a working hypothesis.

2. Be aware that you have a part of yourself that watches and analyzes. Don't fret over what part that is, simply assign it the role of Observer and get to work.

3. Research what it means to set appropriate limits. Ask friends who have children, ask ministers, ask librarians to recommend books. Read up on healthy child rearing and see what should have been the case for you.

4. When you see yourself beginning to set limits and give permissions to your Inner Children in new ways, recognize that the Grownup is beginning to function.

5. Give yourself a wonderful treat each time you recognize the Grownup exercising appropriate authority.

The following story concerning Jose illustrates the kind of dynamic that we see frequently when an Inner Child is in the driver's seat. As you read it, you can get a sense of Jose's Observer at work as he examines his behavior. You can also hear the Grownup beginning to set limits.

Jose's Story

Jose had worked for the Federal Government for 25 years. Keeping a low profile, he had navigated through the bureaucratic system, and had managed to create a secure niche and fairly satisfying work for himself. His three children were in college. He had an attractive sense of humor, was an excellent listener, and gave liberally of his time listening caringly to his wife and others. His sensitivity and ability to empathize, even with situations in which he had no direct experience, attracted people to him.

Even so, he was experiencing difficulties in his personal life. Like most people who have an Inner Child in the driver's seat, Jose was almost completely identified with one of his Inner Children, unable to distinguish between the Children and the Grownup. When this Inner Child was in control, Jose exhibited one or more of four traits: (1) Negativity: Jose avoided any appearance of enthusiasm. Even in his best moments, he tended to be critical, and his compliments were few and far between. In ordinary times, he complained frequently. (2) Moodiness: When Jose failed to get the attention his Inner Child wanted, he brooded, agitated, and sulked silently for days at a time. (3) Competitiveness: This Inner Child competed for attention against others, including his own children. (4) Withholding: Despite his empathic gifts, Jose seldom contributed to the care or training of his children.

The crisis that brought him into therapy was his wife's ultimatum: Change your behavior or go. Jose wasn't happy with this situation, but decided to use the pressure to help himself start facing up to his negative traits.

In therapy, Jose told of his upbringing—how his father was always angry and often physically punitive, how his mother wanted to please yet couldn't protect him from his father. He told of how his wife objected to his controlling behavior, "Your moodiness and unreasonable demands for attention are more than I want to live with for the rest of my life."

Jose: I don't want to upset my wife. On the other hand, I feel what I feel, I'm entitled to my feelings, and I don't see any reason to stifle myself when I'm in my own house. I want her to take care of herself. When I'm good and ready to come back to so-called normal, I'll do it.

Coach: What I'm hearing are Inner Children. Although the reasoning and the voice may sound adult, I don't hear a Grownup.

Jose: I don't get these Inner Children

Coach: Do you feel angry and sad?

Jose: Yes

Coach: Do you feel young, small, and sad?

Jose: (Nods.) But what does that have to do with the here and now?

Coach: In the here and now, those feelings are being generated in your body by one or more Inner Children who are not really living in the here and now, in a way. They're caught in a time capsule. The only person who can reach back into that time capsule to relieve their sadness and pain is your Grownup. You know, the easiest way not to deal with something or someone is to say they don't

exist. How about you listening to your Inner Children, making the
assumption that they're there, and truly hearing them? Take it as
a given that they do exist and go from there.

Jose: Well, I guess there's not that much to lose . . . maybe some time
. . . and some pride.

Jose left the session with an early draft of this book to read and a promise
to finish it within the week. Here, in his own words, is the story of his
breakthrough.

I was taking a shower one day, and I just felt like I never wanted
to get out of the shower. So I sat down, and in a little while, I found
myself in the middle of a bath. As I was lying there in the warm
water, I started thinking, "Why do I feel so resentful and uncaring
toward people I'm close to? Why is it that I act so mean? Why don't
I want to take care of other people?

"There must be one part of me that grew up being criticized and
treated meanly, and that's what that part learned to do—criticize
and treat other people meanly. So this Inner Child is doing what
was done to him.

"He must be angry. He won't take care of anyone else because
nobody took care of him back then. And he's really not being taken
care of now. So he refuses to take care of anyone else."

That made sense, but as I lay thinking, it seemed there had to be
more to it. After all, lots of people aren't very well taken care of by
their parents and they don't resent taking care of others—in fact,
they refuse to be like their parents and they take care of other
people all the time. And they do lots of things to grow, workshops
and the like. I like to do those things too. I've done them in the past,
and I've taken care of myself in the past.

"So," I thought, "What's stopping me from taking care of this
Inner Child? If my Grownup is willing to take care of this Child,
either the Child is unwilling to be taken care of, or there must be
another Inner Child who won't allow the Grownup to take care of
the first one. It must believe that if I start taking care of the first
Inner Child, then my parents will know that they don't have to do
it, they'll never change, and this second Inner Child believes he will
never get taken care of the way he wanted to in the past.

"This second Inner Child, who's not allowing the Grownup to
take care of the first one, hasn't said good-bye to my parents. He's
caught in a time warp. He still believes that my parents—and now

my wife—have to do the caretaking, that I can't survive otherwise, and that if they see me doing it for myself, they'll never help. So this Child continually acts helpless and gets angry when other people don't treat him as if he's weak. And my wife and others do take care of him a lot.

"However, I, the Grownup, am not happy with having other people take care of me, because it's *never enough*. It never feels good all the way through."

So I began talking to this little kid so he could learn his belief wasn't correct any more. "We don't need my parents or my wife to take care of us any more. We're alive; we already survived. But we don't feel that good. The only way it's going to feel good all the way through is when I, the Grownup, do the caretaking. You need to let that happen. And you'll feel a lot better."

As I was talking, I began to feel stronger, and then this little kid started to cry, and so did I. He really didn't want anyone else to take care of him in the here and now. He really wanted me, the Grownup to do it. It was incredible. And I felt very close to him. It became obvious that his ratty behavior was a call for love, which, even though it was misdirected, I could respond to, and I could also make sure that he didn't inflict it on other people. It was going to cost me my marriage if he did.

Why did I have this breakthrough now? Who knows? I don't—maybe it's just the right time for the Grownup to do it.

Since then, I haven't been as regular about talking with him as I should, but I know that will change. It will take some reminding and some practice, but now I know what I have to do, and I will be doing it.

7

The Myth of the Bad Child

Defusing Inner Sibling Rivalry

As Inner Family Healing work progresses, we normally find that clients have assigned responsibility for certain negative behaviors to one or more Inner Children, labeled those Children "bad" or "evil," and then disassociated from them through the use of certain compulsive or addictive behaviors. They then think, "If only I could get rid of this Inner Child, my problems would be over." The following client quote is typical:

> I feel as if there's a monster inside me that wants to degrade and destroy me. The moment I think I have my eating under control, this monster takes over and before I know it I've eaten enough to keep me sleepless for hours, exhausted the next day, and depressed. That's not me, that's something else! If only I could kill it off!

This is distorted Inner Child thinking: There are no inherently evil or bad Inner Children. The Inner Children we've labeled "bad" are hurting and disruptive because their needs are being ignored, and they're doing the best they can to call attention to their distress. We call such Inner Children, Rejected Children.

The part of us who does the blaming and rejecting is most commonly another Inner Child, whom we call the Blamer or the Blaming Child. The Inner Child who operates as the Blamer is very often the same Inner Child who masquerades as the Grownup. The Grownup still exists, of course, but until it develops the knowledge and strength required to care properly for the Inner Children, they remain trapped in an escalating power struggle. The Blaming Child berates and withholds from the Rejected Child, while the Rejected Child retreats further and further, co-opting enormous portions of energy, flooding the person's whole body with depression and fear, and finally turning against the body to create illness.

Since we cannot feel whole as long as we are rejecting either of these Inner Children, healing requires us to search out what drives this power struggle and learn to redirect that energy into other channels. Where battles between the Inner Children are raging, the Grownup needs to be empowered so it can bring both Inner Children lovingly into line. This chapter addresses that challenge in three sections:

1. *What the power struggle looks like from the outside* explains repressions and addictions that accompany Inner Child power struggles and gives examples of what those struggles look like from the outside.

2. *The inside story on the power struggle* explains briefly some of the internal mechanisms of the power struggle and the accompanying addictions.

3. *The strategy for interrupting the power struggle* is based on the fact that when we know the origin of any behavior, we can see the response as positive, in that it may have been the best survival decision a young person could make in a difficult situation. Because the need for love and protection is the driving force and because the Inner Children are intelligent enough to prefer living in a way that works for today, they tend to be willing to adopt new ways of operating when they know the Grownup is truly committed to and capable of ensuring their well-being.

What the Power Struggle Looks Like from the Outside

Two main types of visible behaviors signal the presence of an internal power struggle. In order of intensity, they are as follows:

1. **Repressions:** *A person avoids or pushes down normal responses* in the mistaken belief that they are bad, weak, or inconsistent with their identity and typically substitutes other behaviors to com-

pensate. For example, men who avoid tears may get very angry instead.

2. **Addictions:** *A person engages in an activity to numb or distract from internal pain.* For the purposes of this book, we're going to define an addiction as *any mood-altering activity used repeatedly to numb oneself or otherwise avoid dealing effectively with emotional reality.*

In the past, most people have understood the word addiction only in reference to substance abuse—alcohol and drugs. Today, fortunately, addiction is understood to apply far more broadly. John Bradshaw, in *Bradshaw: On the Family,* puts it very well:

> Our addictions and our compulsivities . . . are our ways of managing our feelings. This is most apparent in experiences that are euphoric, like using alcohol, drugs, sex . . . It is not so obvious in activities which are used to distract from emotions, such as working, buying, gambling, watching television, and thinking obsessively. These are mood altering nonetheless.

Gerald May, M.D., author of the brilliant, must-read book, *Addiction and Grace,* makes the distinction between having strong feelings about something and being addicted to it, by listing five characteristics that must be present for something to qualify as an addiction.* Even after narrowing the definition, he is able to list 115 "attraction addictions" and 80 "aversion addictions," and he considers the list only partial. May further writes, "If it is any consolation, I am addicted to at least fourteen of the listed items, and I could add several others if I wanted to be completely candid, which I do not."

Our ability to understand this wider spectrum of behaviors

---

* According to May, addiction applies to anything where your relationship to it includes five characteristics: (1) tolerance for increasing use; (2) withdrawal symptoms (sustained upset when you can't get it qualifies as a withdrawal symptom); (3) self-deception (denial that there's any problem); (4) distortion of attention (preoccupation with doing or not doing it); and (5) loss of willpower (inability to withstand the impulse toward the addictive behavior).

as addictive makes available to us decades of wisdom accumulated by hundreds of thousands of recovering addicts.

Based on our experience, we divide addictions into two categories:

a. *Self-abuse:* A person abuses one's own body and mind through substance (food, drugs), activity (overwork), painful relationships (usually involving compulsive caretaking), or internal processes such as compulsive thinking or compulsive self-criticism.

Self-abuse normally serves one of two purposes: (1) the outside or surface pain distracts attention from the deeper inner pain, or (2) the evident distress created usually evokes guilt, pity, or praise rather than criticism from abusive caretakers.

b. *Abuse of others:* A person abuses others using criticism and guilt-pushing, rejection, rage, ridicule, double-talk, or physical or sexual attack. At one end of the scale, this can be the person who enters a room looking for something or someone to criticize. At the other end are the rapists and mass murderers whose rage is so global that nothing outside themselves has any value except as an object for destruction.

Driving the repeated denigration of self or others is the need to create an illusion of power, which helps us deny the sense of helplessness that still haunts us from the past. To put it another way, one or more Inner Children are addicted to rage, violence, and power, because it not only helps them temporarily escape inner pain, but gives them the illusion they can control whatever surface or outer element they blame for causing or adding to the pain.

These two behavior patterns are progressive; that is:

1. To the extent that we repress ourselves to conceal or avoid dealing with our internal pain and fear, we create additional pain.

2. If we continue to create more pain through repression, we'll eventually feel the need to adopt another mechanism that numbs us to the original pain we're not dealing with plus the additional pain we're creating. This behavior, if pursued, becomes an addiction with its own demands and a life of its own.

This creates even more pain, which makes us doubly uncomfortable.

3. We invariably begin to take it out on others, directly or indirectly.

   You've heard it said' that what people do to others, they eventually do to themselves. It's also true that what people do to themselves, they eventually inflict on others.

To determine if you have an addictive behavior pattern or not, ask these questions:

1. Can I quit if I choose to?
2. Will I quit?
3. What is it costing me to have this behavior pattern? What am I getting out of it?
4. What do people who love me say about this behavior pattern?

For those of us who until now have understood "addiction" to apply only to substance abuse, here are some illustrations showing the wider range of what addictive power struggles look like from the outside.

Example of Repression

One of the most common examples of repression is the man who avoids sadness and tears because he considers them to be unmanly and substitutes work or anger instead. Sad men suffer greatly because of their unwillingness to provide their Inner Children with the time and tenderness they need in order to mourn. Here's an example.

A kind man, Rob was reared by an abusive father who ridiculed him for crying in hurt. At about age 6, he made the decision to be strong—to be a *man*, to show no one his tears—in fact, not even to feel them himself. Rob didn't cry for years, not even at 19 when his parents died in a car crash. But Rob did occasionally feel teary, and when he did, he felt very awkward. He would then allot a very limited time for feeling whatever sadness he felt and then say to himself, "That's more than enough time, it's time to shape up, you're getting in my way. What's the matter with you, for God's sake. Do you want to cry your whole life away?"—and so on.

Later, as a father of a young son, he found he was experiencing depression and a great deal of sadness. When his own young son cried, Rob didn't know how to react—he either behaved as if his son's tears signaled enormous sorrow and needed major comforting, or he acted irritated and drew away as if his son were doing something wrong when he cried. In both cases, he was projecting onto his son and overreacting to his own sorrow, which he himself had not expressed for all those years. As happens in all families, Rob's biological child evoked for Rob all the unresolved sadness of his own Inner Children.

What it cost Rob to suppress his sadness was his ability to be close and accepting of himself and his son when either of them felt sad. What a price! He was also teaching his son that no one could be comfortably close to a person in pain.

When he began Inner Family healing work, Rob at first decided that the Inner Child who needed to cry was actually the source of his problems. He would say something like, "Crying is stupid. It doesn't solve anything. If it weren't for this Inner Child, I wouldn't have any problems. There's something really wrong with this Child."

Eventually, when Rob began to take in accurate information about crying and how it relates to being a man, he began to allow himself the time and a place to cry. Each time he did so, Rob learned afresh that nothing was wrong with his Inner Child. The Child was just a little boy, and by forbidding him his tears, Rob was simply replicating the painful situation that had created the inner pain to begin with. Rob eventually came to relish his freedom to cry, because it made him more open to all feelings, including joy. Moreover, it opened the gateway of honesty between him and his son, bringing them closer than they'd ever been.

People suppress not only sadness but also fear and anger: Fear particularly is judged by both men and women as childish, so when a man feels fear, he'll likely express anger instead. Women, on the other hand, will go more often to tears and sadness to escape fear. As a result, both men and women often fail to get the information, assistance, and reassurance required to allay their fears. Many people of both genders judge anger as being negative; when they repress anger, they create distance in relationships and depression in their own bodies.

To the extent we refuse to express any of our emotions, we forfeit the joy that is rightfully ours in simply being alive. Suppressing tears always perpetuates an inner sadness, which then colors the rest of life. Suppressing anger robs us of peace and the right to relax and it eats away at our physical bodies.

In cases of repression, the part that restricts self-expression is often the Inner Grownup operating on erroneous information. This is good news because, once given correct information and encouragement, the person usually changes behavior quickly and easily. All the Inner Children need is someone to give permission, to say, "Yes that's OK to do, I'll protect you if anything comes up," and when the Grownup does so, they're all ready to go.

However, when the oppressor is a not a Grownup but an Inner Child, behavioral changes can take more effort and intention to achieve. The person's behavior is more likely to be an addiction with a life and drive of its own. This is the kind of pattern we're going to deal with in the rest of this chapter.

Examples of Addiction to Self-Abuse

Self-abuse is often difficult to identify as an addiction because society actually approves of martyrdom in various forms and because our ability to distinguish healthy from unhealthy self-sacrifice is impaired. Self-sacrifice can be a healing miracle; too often, however, a persistent pattern of taking abuse has less to do with enlightened self-sacrifice than with the Inner Child's need to control another person. For example, the Inner Child may want to keep a parent from leaving or hurting them or the Child may want a reason for staying angry to keep them at a distance. Let's look at addiction to self-abuse through the experience of "Mack."

> Mack had a history of going into one painful relationship after another and ending all of them feeling wronged, righteous, and vindicated in his belief that women are dishonest, vindictive, and full of hate for men.
>
> One part of the problem was that Mack kept choosing women who had significant unresolved rage at men in general, and no compunction about taking it out on him in particular. Another part of the problem was that Mack didn't feel entitled or safe enough to protect himself against a woman, especially one who cooked for him (like his mother did) and seemed particularly powerful. Instead, when Mack first felt angry about something (when it's usually most constructive to communicate), he would repress his thoughts and feelings. He didn't believe he had the right to voice

and enforce a protest until he had "sufficient cause." As his abuse went on, Mack would complain, but he wouldn't put any energy into actually changing the situation. He felt he had to wait until the woman finally stepped beyond the invisible line he'd drawn for her to cross; then, when she had abused him enough, he felt justified in putting his foot down. However, by the time he finally felt entitled to express his rage, he was so angry that he couldn't be constructive. He couldn't deal with the tremendous rush of adrenalin that flooded his system. Instead, he would abruptly abandon the woman without either warning or regret of any kind. After it was all over, he would feel depressed, abandoned, and lost. Even so, when he came out of that phase, Mack simply found another woman, even more abusive, who his Blaming Child could make wrong and attack.

During the latest relationship, however, Mack finally connected with his angry Inner Children and so did his woman friend. Both of them are currently learning about the collusion that goes on between their Inner Children, and they've made a commitment to keep their Grownups present. Progress is good. As of this writing, they have jointly purchased a house that they've been living in for a year and a half.

Examples of Addiction to Abusing Others

Abuse of others can take many forms, both overt and covert. The common denominator is a person's adamant and relentless determination to exercise power over others as a way of numbing themselves to their own pain and denying past helplessness. Sometimes it also includes a desire to punish the world for their own pain. Here are two examples.

Katie was a rage-aholic. She walked around in her family just one step from a screaming tantrum, and her children and husband never knew just what would set her off. They walked on eggs, and would go to great lengths not to provoke her. As counselors in the field of addiction can attest, this kind of pattern can be as addictive as heroin, and as fatal.

Another example of both emotional and physical cruelty is Tommy, a hemophiliac teenager. Normal play was dangerous for him, since the slightest blow could start him bleeding, send him to the hospital, and even kill him. Other children were cautioned never to hurt Tommy in any way. He lived in a building where all the children were several years younger than he, and he used his seniority and his disability to tyrannize the children in the building. Like most such personalities, he was able to enlist a local bully, a dullard with a mean streak, to "capture" children on their way home. The bully would bring them as "prisoners" into Tommy's room, where he would force them to act out torture and perversions. To terrorize the children into complying with his wishes, he would physically torture and kill cats and then mock the children for crying and being frightened and upset. Tommy is dead now but the children he tortured still carry the scars of his cruelty in their adult lives.

The most difficult categories of covert abuse of others to identify are silent. Jose, the civil servant described in the case study at the end of chapter 6, was a silent abuser. Silent abuse takes many forms: sulking, withholding approval, deliberately ignoring or nonverbally rejecting another's overtures, and exuding anger. This last is the most difficult, because it occurs more on an energy level than in observable behavior: It's the kind of thing that people who are sensitive feel when they say things like, "I can tell when she's in the house—the whole atmosphere feels heavy and dark. It's not like that when she's not there." Even though this kind of behavior is silent, it is nevertheless abusive and the abusers usually know what they're doing.

That's how some Inner Sibling struggles look to others. What goes on internally is quite different: No matter what form of abuse we're discussing, what abusers may or may not realize is, when they hurt others, they simultaneously inflict the same damage on themselves internally, which brings us to the important dynamics of the power struggle.

The Inside Story on the Power Struggle

From the inside, the power struggle between the Blaming and the Rejected Children looks all too familiar: It's the Family Spell all over again. Here's how it starts: The Blaming Child says "No one will ever do that to me again," chooses the power position, and begins to reject all signs of vulnerability in themselves and others. The Blaming Child's intent in assuming the position of power is to make himself invulnerable to threats to his psychological or physical survival. He can thus avoid the position of victim and the pain of his own suffering, past and present. The Blamer also tends to reject or criticize signs of vulnerability in others, because it reminds him of the vulnerability in himself. The problem is, the younger, vulnerable Rejected Child is still around, still carrying pain from the situations depicted in the Family Spell. That Child never goes away and never grows up. Moreover, the longer the Rejected Child is denied, deprived, and abused, the more strongly it presses to express its needs and the pain associated with the deprivation.

To deal with this continuing and increasing pressure from the Rejected Child, the Blaming Child begins to employ behaviors that deaden pain by flooding the body with some kind of mood-altering chemical. This can be some kind of ingested substance, or it can be the adrenalin produced by excitement, fear, anxiety, stress, or anger.

This chemical gives only temporary relief, because until the feelings are expressed and the Rejected Child begins getting his true needs met, the source of the pressure never goes away permanently. On the contrary, the pressure keeps building.

To cope with this increasing pressure, the Blaming Child employs more and more of the pain-killing behaviors. Eventually, the pain-killing mechanism itself becomes the primary focus, and all other parts of the person, including both the Blaming and the Rejected Child, are sacrificed to its maintenance. So if alcohol is what we engage in to avoid dealing with pain, we eventually put our drinking before all else, sacrificing our work, our health, our families, our happiness. If painting is what we engage in to avoid dealing with pain, we eventually put our painting work before all else, even when we think we don't.

Instead of liberating us, our pain-killer has become our jailer. The thing to which the Blaming Child is addicted becomes an idol, a god to us, and we sacrifice on its altar everything else we hold dear.

Even more ironic and distressing: Because of the way the Family Spell operates, the pattern of addiction tends to replicate the abuse pattern experienced in the original family setting. If we're looking for a way to kill our pain, we usually pick from the array of options our parents showed us. If they worked addictively, we work addictively. If they were rage-aholics, we may be rage-aholics, too, or we may never show anger and marry angry people instead. Some of us think we'll beat the system by choosing the opposite of what our parents did: If they worked obsessively, we may refuse to work, insisting others work endlessly to take care of us instead. If they drank, we may be teetotalers—and marry drunks instead. But in either case, whether we imitate or reject our parents' patterns, we remain preoccupied with the addiction. Thus, as maintaining the power position becomes more and more compelling to us, we sacrifice the well-being of our younger Inner Children in just the same ways that our parents did.

When examining what perpetuates the power struggle, when we're grown, one is tempted to finger the Blaming Child as the sole culprit, but in fact, both the Blamer and the Rejected Child play a part. The Rejected Child in us can be as addicted as the Blamer, but to the safety of being invisible, insignificant, and impotent rather than angry or controlling. That repressed or depressive position feels safe for two reasons: First, it keeps energy low, which in the Inner Child's frame of reference may avoid attracting dangerous attention to herself from others. Second, being the helpless Victim enables this Inner Child to shift all responsibility to the Blamer and thus protects her from the danger of doing something the original parents would have attacked. Paradoxically, the Blamer's constant abuse keeps the Rejected Child "safe" by feeding the Rejected Child's addiction to being controlled.

Strategy for Interrupting the Power Struggle

Our basic strategy for interrupting the power struggle between the Blaming Child and the Rejected Child has three main parts:

1. Educate and strengthen the Grownup.
2. Judge the behavior, not the Inner Children.
3. Devise alternative means to achieve the positive intent underlying the behavior.

Educate and Strengthen the Grownup

In chapter 6, "Empowering the Reluctant Grownup," we outlined a strategy for strengthening and empowering an underdeveloped Grownup. We cannot overemphasize the importance of this step, and we urge you to reread that chapter.

In addition, we strongly recommend, if you are committed to healing addictions, that you join a community of people with similar objectives. The 12-step programs that have proliferated throughout this country in the last 5 years now offer such a variety of styles and focuses that most people can find a group meeting that suits their needs exactly. There's little that can match the healing power of a community dedicated to mutual support.

What the group will do is offer collective wisdom on the next two parts of the healing strategy.

Judge the Behavior, Not the Inner Child

The task of loving often boils down to **loving who a person is, while refusing to condone unacceptable behavior.** This is much easier said and done at a distance, of course. The closer we get to people and the more impact their behavior has upon our own person, the more difficult or impossible the task may appear, because it looks like people are what they do. Let's look at this more closely, because we all have trouble with it.

Although behavioral or thinking patterns are distinct from being; they *affect* a person's being profoundly: Repeated, prolonged behaviors that denigrate or wound oneself or others will line one's face, rob one of vitality and creativity, blind one to possibilities, and strengthen obsessions and self-hate. Similarly, loving and caring for others produces beauty in a person's face and life. It's possible there's a point of no return, where behavior and being aren't separate—people like Hitler and Idi Amin may have passed a certain point where they got to *be* what they did. Nevertheless, *in any case where the person truly desires healing, we are convinced the Inner Children remain available and healing is possible.*

So how do we separate the Inner Child from his evil behavior so we can love unconditionally? How can we access our own compassion for a part of ourselves or others we see as uncooperative, destructive, or otherwise unlovable?

First, we need to see that even the most horrifying behavior arises from a need for love. Deep within the Inner Family, there are desperately hurting Inner Children, whose panic and isolation are vast. Here's an example that may shed light on this:

> I remember in a mental hospital a little three-year-old who, because of cancer on one side of his face, looked like Beauty and the Beast in one package. He was there because he had attempted to kill his little six-month old sister.
>
> What positive intent could one possibly find underlying such an act? What I learned was that the parents were ordinary folk who had cut him off emotionally because they could not cope with his illness and the way he was dying. One day, he was brought home from yet another stint in the hospital, and there was a new baby in

the crib that had been his. All he saw was that this new baby had stolen all the love that used to be his. If only the baby would go away, perhaps his parents would love him again.

Working on this assumption, the medical staff lavished love, caring, and holding on this little one for over 6 months. It worked: Insofar as was possible in his situation, he became an ordinary 3-year-old. He was then given to a warm and loving foster family. For the last 6 months of his life, he was truly happy.

Based on cases like this, our working assumption is that there is goodness in every person. We believe every child is born into the world preferring love over hate, trust over suspicion, truth over falsehood, openness over secrecy, life over death. All persistently unacceptable behavior arises from early lack of unconditional physical care and love. The earlier and more severe that early deprivation is, the more pronounced the negative behavior tends to be. Those Inner Children have chosen that behavior as a defense against what is or appears to be an even greater evil to self or others. For example, we can grow up in such a terrible environment that we decide the best way to survive is to hurt others first so they don't dare try to kill us. The thought may be, "I'm safe as long as I can hurt people." To such a person, *not* hurting someone can feel terribly threatening.

Sometimes, even with an understanding of these inner dynamics, it seems impossible to love our Inner Children who sometimes seem bent on our own destruction. To do so, we must discover and align ourselves with their positive intent.

Devise Alternative Means to Achieve Positive Intent

Healthy, normal preferences persist unless the Child learns through experience that they are too dangerous, painful, or costly and devises another way to get its needs met. Even then, we believe an underlying preference for the healthy persists. If a person's Inner Children can learn to see there's a better way to achieve a healthy intent, they choose it. To help them do that, you need to: (1) identify the positive intent, and then (2) magnify your own capacity for loving them as the major way to free them to choose a better way.

Identify the Positive Intent

You can often discover Inner Children's positive intent simply by asking them why they do something or what would happen if they didn't do it. For example, here are some positive intentions discovered from just a few Inner Children we've worked with:

- A little girl found it dangerous to tell the truth in her family because family members attacked anyone who threatened to reveal the family secrets. Attacked often and severely enough, she eventually panicked at the idea of telling even a simple truth and lied compulsively instead. No one has a good enough memory to be a compulsive liar, so this caused other problems, which led in turn to more lying and other types of dishonest behavior.

   The positive intent here was to protect her family and herself from whatever danger it was that they feared.

- A little boy learned that it was painful and scary to love his dad. His father was an alcoholic who one day would hug him and the next day beat him up for no reason. He decided since it was too painful to love his father, it was probably too painful to love anyone, and so he chose to live his life on excitement instead of love. Over a period of time, this became a biological addiction to adrenalin, which translated into crisis-oriented living. He eventually married an alcoholic, became one himself, had a rags-to-riches relationship with his job, played cops-and-robbers, and even today must be vigilant in order not to create conflict and danger in otherwise ordinary tranquil situations.

   The positive intent here was to provide protection from the father's inconsistency. If he shut down, then although he had to do without the love, at least he had less direct pain and had what looked like an exciting life.

- A little girl learned it was costly to tell someone what she wanted because her older sisters often used that information to hurt her by withholding that thing or by demanding something far greater in return. Her father struggled at three different jobs, and she didn't feel good about adding to his burden. So she decided she wouldn't tell anyone what she wanted. In fact, she had just about decided never to need anything. This was very self-destructive, for needs are real, and by refusing to acknowledge and meet them directly, she gave herself no option except doing without or manipulating others to give her what she needed without either acknowledging the giver or feeling fully satisfied with what she got.

This pattern is very common to men: a little boy who's decided never to have needs will marry a nurturer who perceives the Child's deep needs and takes care of them as best she can. However, he will be unable to acknowledge her gifts to him because if he did, then it would prove that he does need, and that would feel too dangerous to his Inner Child. So when she asks for thanks or for nurture in return, he will reject and punish her instead for trying to expose the truth.

The positive intent behind this pattern is to protect oneself from others' abuse, to be independent, and to avoid burdening a father who was already overworked.

These examples illustrate that it's possible to think about positive intent no matter what the overt behavior. The Inner Children know what positive intent lies behind most actions. When they let the Grownup in on it, the Grownup can move to provide alternative means to satisfy the same intent.

Magnify the Capacity for Loving

The alternative means required to achieve the positive intent these Inner Children are reaching for can almost always be expressed in terms of love and approval, both of which can be amply supplied by the Inner Grownup. Accordingly, an important part of Inner Family Healing involves connecting with and expanding our Grownup's capacity to feel loving and protective toward the Inner Children. For some people, connecting with one's loving feelings is easy, but for many of us, especially if we're going through severe crisis or are depressed, it's not easy at all.

How do you love yourself if you're so sure you're unlovable that you dare not feel any warm feelings toward anyone or anything? There are two possibilities here. First, it's possible you have loving feelings that you simply don't recognize as such. The other is that you have shut down so far that you cannot feel love at all.

Recognizing Loving Feelings for What They Are

It's more common than you might expect to have a great deal of affection and care for certain things or people and not recognize those feelings and behaviors as love. Any positive, expanded, or comfortably relaxed feeling, no matter how faint it is, is a part of what we call love. Love's opposites are fear and indifference. If you're one of the people who isn't sure what love feels like, here's an exercise that will help you label those feelings accurately:

First, place yourself in a comfortable position, sitting or lying down.

Then take three or four deep breaths and ask yourself the following questions out loud. Even better, have someone you trust ask the questions.

After you hear each question, pause for a few seconds, breathe deeply once or twice, and then answer Yes or No. If you have someone else asking the questions, they should say, "Pause. . . Breathe. . .and respond." If your answer is not a clear No, then answer Yes.

Do you love food when you're hungry?
(Pause, breathe, & answer, yes or no.)
Do you love feeling good?
(Pause, breathe, etc.)
Do you love fresh air?
Do you love the idea of flying?
Do you love to run?
Do you love to dance?
Do you love nature?
The sea? a beautiful running stream?
Sky?
Moon?
Sunshine on your body?
Wind in your hair?
(Remember to pause and breathe after each one)
Do you love dogs? puppies?
Do you love cats? Do you love animals? Do you love colors? Do you love music? Do you love houses? Do you love sports?—baseball, football, fishing?

Accessing Loving Feelings When There Seem To Be None

If you have trouble connecting with a positive experience of loving, it may be because you see life and the world as war and a battlefield or a desperate struggle to stay alive in a treacherous jungle. No doubt, that has something to do with your experience.

The question is whether you are willing to see the world in a different way. (Not able, *willing*.) It's true that this world does contain dangers and terrible things do happen, but one cannot open up to self and others without knowing some other truths that are equally relevant to our survival. Specifically, the Grownup needs to understand the following:

There was a time when you knew love because it flowed through you to all those around you. Babies are born loving. It's a capacity that accompanies their ability to feel pleasure in their bodies—even if they are in considerable pain, they feel the goodness of being held by a loving person. You yourself know, when you've just experienced the pleasure of a good meal or sleep, you feel less irritable, frightened, or depressed, and you feel more positive toward yourself and those around you.

When you stopped loving or couldn't remember having loved, it was because that love was neither received nor returned. Instead, you may have experienced abuse, fear, neglect, or abandonment from those responsible for your care.

That wouldn't be such a big problem were it not for the fact that you thought it was your fault that you were treated that way. Newborn babies have no boundaries. They experience themselves as one with the universe; they don't yet sense themselves as separate from their mother or anything else. Because of this, they believe everything in the world happens because of them—even though they aren't yet sure how it happens. They cry and mother feeds them, picks them up. It's like the story of the white mice in the laboratory cage: One mouse says to the other, "It's easy. I've got this big dumb guy trained. All I have to do is tap this bar over here and he forks out food." That's the way babies think. So when you were a baby, if someone hurt you, you believed that you actually made that happen, even though you couldn't say how or why you'd do such a thing.

Your inner children still believe, consciously or unconsciously, that because someone hurt or neglected them, there's something wrong with them. Your Grownup doesn't know any better either. The information is missing from your system. No wonder you won't let yourself feel love: It's too dangerous to get close to someone else. If they get close to you, they'll find out why other people hurt you and they'll hurt you too—or leave you, which may feel even worse.

So you're not different, because everybody feels this way to some degree, not only about their childhood, but about present-day difficulties. One of the biggest problems rape victims have is getting over the idea that they were somehow accomplices in their own abuse. We have all experienced hurts that we mistakenly believe were our fault. If you feel different or have had trouble getting in touch with loving feelings, you probably had a rougher time of it when you were little, thought that you were worse than other people, and experienced getting close as especially threatening.

The truth is, although the expression of love can be blocked, love can't be killed. It is, quite literally, the stuff of which we are made.

Taking in these ideas can be especially difficult for people with a history of childhood sexual abuse. Sexual abuse represents such a fundamental violation of the trust relationship to which any child is entitled that most survivors of sexual abuse fear or reject any relationships where trust is called for, including love relationships. In the next chapter, we turn to this very important subject of child sexual abuse.

8

Healing Sexually Abused Inner Children

The number of people who were sexually abused as children is stagger-ing. The most conservative estimate we've come across is 20 percent of the population. Highly sophisticated, random surveys of general populations have ranged from 38 percent of 900 women in San Francisco to 22 percent nationally (27 percent of women, 16 percent of men) in a sample of 2,627. In the United States, that represents almost 40 million adults.* The conse-quences are costly and heartbreaking. Experts generally agree that sexual abuse begets sexual abuse: one such expert asserts that all incarcerated abusers with whom he has worked came from a history of severe sexual and physical abuse. The Rader Institute, specializing in eating disorders, reports that 85 percent of their parents have been sexually abused as children.

Given these appalling statistics, it isn't surprising that Inner Children often reveal that they've been sexually abused.

It's only common sense to obtain competent professional treatment in such cases: Often the trauma is too severe for a layperson to explore safely, especially if the issue comes up before a person's Grownup has developed the necessary strength to deal with it. Even if good professional treatment is hard to find, we strongly recommend you persevere in the search.

In the meantime, while no book can substitute for competent profes-

---

* Crewdson, John, *Sexual Abuse of Children in America:* Little, Brown & Company, 1988

sional treatment, we want you to understand enough about the subject of sexual abuse to:

- Recognize indicators that sexual abuse is what you're dealing with
- Keep the door to treatment open by honoring the cues and reassuring the Inner Children that it's safe to speak about the abuse, instead of slamming it shut by unwittingly signaling them that this subject is — still — taboo
- Make reasoned choices about getting needed help.

To those ends, this chapter: (1) describes indications that a person may have been sexually abused as a child; (2) defines sexual abuse and the conspiracy of silence that perpetuates it; (3) outlines the strategy we've used in sexual abuse cases; (4) invites sexual child abuse victims who are themselves molesting children to try Inner Family Healing as a means of arresting this addictive behavior; and (5) offers two accounts of Inner Family Healing written by two clients of ours who were sexually abused as children.

Indications a Person May Have Been Sexually Abused as a Child

If the memory of child sexual abuse is partially or entirely buried, how does one tell if early sexual abuse is a problem? Ultimately, the Inner Children tell, but they won't let the secret out until they're very sure we are trustworthy. Until then, there are usually a whole variety of clues that seem initially to be unrelated and unfounded, but that later turn out to be entirely significant.

Here is an extensive list of characteristics exhibited by adult victims of child sexual abuse.*

- Difficulty in forming positive sexual relationships; inability to

---

* Olio, Karen A. *Retrieval and Utilization of Memories in the Treatment of Adult Survivors of Sexual Abuse*: Unpublished paper, 1988. We thank Ms. Olio for some of the following indicators.

enjoy lovemaking, even with someone dearly loved; a habit of picking partners who one doesn't especially like or feel comfortable around

- Fear of allowing others to get emotionally close
- Eating disorders, both overeating and anorexia and bulimia; both men and women, but especially very pretty women, may build a wall of fat to keep others from being sexually attracted to them
- Wearing far more clothes than called for by the occasion or the weather, e.g., refusing to take off a coat when it's hot
- Anger or disgust at one's gender
- Promiscuity, sexual addictiveness, preoccupation with sex
- Fear of sex
- Impotence; inability to reach orgasm.
- Chronic rage at members of the opposite sex; punitive use of sexuality in relationships
- Failure to protect themselves from possible sexual attack; attraction to sexually and physically dangerous situations
- Lack of self-esteem
- Dislike of the body
- Withdrawal as a way of life
- Flashbacks to scenes of sexual abuse
- Experiences of arousal connected with
  - Being close to children
  - Experiencing or witnessing violence
  - Experiences of invasion of personal space by another
- Compulsion to engage in sexual behavior with children
- Anger toward young children for expressing their sexuality
- Emotional surges in response to material related to child sexual abuse
- Verbal statements suggesting sexual abuse that "just pop out" in startling ways that seem to be out of context.

Child Sexual Abuse Defined

What is sexual abuse? We define sexual abuse as *any act toward a minor by an adult or older child that exploits the child for one's own sexual gratification.*

What does sexual abuse look like? Forms of sexual abuse range from provocative conversation, to exposure, to fondling, to penetration into any body orifice. The abuse may be painful or pleasurable. It may be forced on the child or the child may participate willingly—after all, all children love to touch and cuddle and play, and normal curiosity about sexuality begins quite early in life. It is almost always accompanied by secrecy.

What makes the act abusive? The adverse consequences of sexual abuse sometimes show up early, but the most severe repercussions become evident as the victim grows into adulthood and tries to form healthy partnerships. Here they are:

- Abusers think solely of their own gratification. They thus teach that in sexual encounters the victim's own interests and well-being count for little or nothing.

- Abuse colors the child's first sexual experience with ambivalence and a sense of shame: If sexual feelings and sensations are OK, says the child, then it shouldn't be necessary for them to be kept secret. Since we have to keep these feelings a secret, they can't be OK.

- Children tend to blame themselves for the abuse instead of placing responsibility with the abusing adult, where it belongs. They believe the reason they were abused is because there is something inherently "bad" about themselves and therefore they must hide their "badness" from others or be rejected. This leads them to withdraw from others, which creates more pain and impedes their ability to heal.

- Being sexually abused as a child creates an unhealthy tendency to bond with exploitive, irresponsible persons. Furthermore, if the abuser is also a parent, the child will have difficulty separating from that parent and won't be free to bond with a mate of similar age.

- Sexual abuse awakens the child's sexuality prematurely, so that it assumes excessive importance in all later interactions with key figures in one's life. Behaviorally, this excessive emphasis on sexuality is usually expressed in an all-or-nothing way. That is, it produces either promiscuity or sexual repression or both, with the person flip-flopping back and forth between the two.

- Early sexual abuse interferes with the development of the ability to keep other people from violating one's personal boundaries. Again, the all-or-nothing pattern seems to apply, with the victim either unable to allow people to get close at all, or unable to prevent it.
- Sexual abuse conditions victims to feel helpless and, to counter that, they often make decisions like "I'll be powerful so no one will ever do that to me again." In expressing that decision later in life, they often assume either the Persecutor or Rescuer position and reenact the abuse. If they assume the Persecutor position, they may become child sexual abusers themselves. It's a known fact that most child sexual abusers were themselves abuse victims. If they assume the Rescuer position, they may end up working on an abuse hotline, or doing foster care work against enormous odds.

On both societal and individual levels, what keeps the problem in place is secrecy.

The Conspiracy of Silence

Our society has engaged for many years in a conspiracy of silence that protects sexual abusers, not the abused. Secrecy is the surest protection for people who lie or distort the truth, and since child sexual abusers consciously or unconsciously lie to get what they want, they create an environment of secrecy to shield themselves from exposure.

Thanks to the media, especially TV talk show hosts and hostesses, the public now is learning how to speak out. Even so, we have a long way to go before the veil of secrecy will be pulled down, for the children themselves have difficulty communicating, even as adults.

The Lies and Half-Truths Abusers Tell Children

Typically, abusers manipulate a child into serving his or her own sexual desires by taking a truth and twisting it. They then protect themselves by convincing the child not to tell anyone what's happening. Here are examples of lies and half-truths that abusers tell children:

— "Good children obey grownups (mostly true) and so they

should always do what grownups ask them to (not always true)"

— "You're so sexy you're *making* me touch you sexually (not true) and if you tell, no one will believe you (possibly true)."

— "This is what people do when they love one another." (Yes, if they are both consenting adults.)

— "If your mother or father knew what you did with me, they'd be very angry (true, but at the abuser, not the child), and they'd never love you again." (false)

— "You **want** me to do this." (Perhaps, but responsible adults have sex with other adults, not with children. Making the decision not to be sexual with a child is an adult responsibility.)

— "This is special treatment for you because you're so pretty, such a good girl/boy. We mustn't tell the others because they'd be jealous." (Perhaps, but it isn't relevant to whether the adult should be doing it or not.)

— "You have to let me touch you sexually because I'm your (father/mother/uncle/grandfather/aunt/grandmother/nur se)." (False. A child doesn't have to let anyone touch them in this way.)

— "If your mother knew, it would kill her." (Not true at all, but little children take such statements literally.)

— "Your parents already know about this. They said it was OK—everybody does it (not true), but they don't want to talk about it." (Perhaps, but no longer as likely to be true as it used to be.)

These lies can stand as truths for the child as long as they remain secret with no one to controvert them.

Why Children Don't Tell

Most children do not tell when they are sexually abused because of threats, adult disbelief and denial, and children's inherent difficulty in communicating the problem, and confusion.

Threats. To keep the child from telling others, sexual abusers may threaten to harm the child or its parents. "If you tell, I'll kill your father or I'll hurt your sister, and it'll be your fault." Younger children, especially, who believe what they're told and who take things very literally, swallow this kind of craziness.

Threats also come from other caretakers in ways that discourage disclosure. An angry demanding parent creates an atmosphere for a child that says, "Whatever you say, you're wrong (not good enough, bad, stupid)." "Don't bother me."

Adult disbelief and denial. Until recently, when children complained of sexual abuse, most adults assumed they were making up stories or just being difficult. There's been an absolute wall of unbelief. In some cases, it's clear we're dealing not with simple disbelief, which can arise from ignorance, but with denial, which has somewhat more sinister roots. For example, some adults may even have a sense of what was going on but refuse to face the possibility. It's not uncommon for the non-abusing spouse to feel some relief that the abusing partner's sexual demands are being taken care of by someone else.

The other reason for denial is that survivors unable to acknowledge sexual abuse in their own lives have trouble acknowledging the existence of sexual abuse anywhere else. *Because they have repressed the memories, many victims act them out instead as adults, by sexually abusing other children.*

The impulse to interact sexually with children isn't confined to actual abusers. A few victims have courageously acknowledged that they experienced arousal toward young children—when babysitting, for example. Although they didn't act on the impulse, they reported having been horrified at themselves. More commonly, victims don't share such feelings openly. Rather, they experience such self-loathing that they deeply repress their memories and cannot bring themselves to acknowledge child sexual abuse in any lives, their own or those of others.

Victims' difficulty in communicating that a problem exists. The assumption that children are lying has exaggerated the natural difficulties most children have in talking about sexual abuse. These difficulties include the following:

1. *Children don't tell the secrets because they don't know how.* They usually do communicate in some way, and the observant, perceptive parent can pick up clues that all is not right. Sometimes the child will exhibit a profound personality change, or develop an intense, apparently irrational aversion to a particular relative or friend of the family.

2. *Children tend to keep abuse a secret because they feel confused about what's really happening.* On the one hand, the child hates what is being done to it: They know the act is exploitive and they feel strange because of the secrecy. They are often forced into participating.

On the other hand, it's normal for a child to enjoy attention and touch from an adult. It's not uncommon to hear an abuse survivor say, "He was my favorite uncle. How could he do that to me?" This is especially true for neglected or battered children; they are most vulnerable because they're so starved for affection. Abusers tend to seek out these needy children because they're so easily manipulated. The abusing adult may look like an oasis of affection, simply because of being willing to make contact. For severely deprived children, even the violent or hurtful abuser may look better than nothing at all.

3. *In their pain, horror, and confusion, the victims cooperate with the conspiracy by repressing the memories.* This repression may insulate the child from shock in childhood, but later impedes healing by depriving the victim of the conscious knowledge they need in order to acknowledge that sexual abuse occurred. What remains unrecognized remains unavailable for healing. These silent victims also have trouble acknowledging the possibility of sexual abuse in others' histories as well, because what they can't acknowledge in their own histories, they tend to deny in others as well.

Recent publicity regarding appalling scandals in day care centers and the courage of people who have told their personal stories of incest and sexual abuse have begun to open the way for a more intelligent approach to the subject. But changes are very slow, and a good deal of evidence suggests that we've only begun to comprehend the dimensions of this epidemic of sexual abuse of minors.

Suggested Strategy for Healing Sexually Abused Inner Children

For the victim, the first door that has to be opened in the healing process is the door of silence. Until the abuser's actions and lies are exposed for examination by informed, responsible adults, the Inner Children will remain trapped inside an unreality. So the basic steps we follow are these:

1. *We build a safe environment so the Inner Children can unburden themselves of the secrets.* Safety consists of permission, protection, and power: Permission to be open without condemnation, protection from punitive influences

(oneself or others), and power to control the situation and implement change. This last item, power to control, is especially important.

Unlike therapy clients who may expect a therapist to "do it for them" and try to turn over all judgment and authority to the therapist, most victims of child sexual abuse need to feel they are in control of the therapy process. They couldn't turn over authority even if they wanted to, because their level of distrust is so high as a result of the abuse. There is always at least one Inner Child who doesn't fully trust anyone but itself.

We support this attitude and make it clear that we don't expect the victim to trust us more than themselves. "You're in charge" and "Trust yourself," two foundations of our process, are particularly important here.

To make explicitly clear that it is the client in whom ultimate power resides, we ask the person to assign a part of themselves to the role of Co-therapist and to participate actively in determining the needs of the Inner Child and direction of therapy. This provides the person with an extra measure of autonomy and control over the situation. During the sessions, we actively involve the Co-therapist by calling Time Out for such things as: conferring about how the Co-therapist sees the process going, asking for suggestions for alternatives, finding out what the Grownup or an Inner Child may be withholding, or seeing if we are missing something. We also use these Time Outs as opportunities for educating the Co-therapist, and, because the Inner Children and the Grownup are always tuning in, they receive the information as well.

2. *We honor cues the Inner Child sends that suggest sexual abuse may have taken place.* It's only human to dismiss or discount information that doesn't fit our current thinking about something. "When in doubt, toss it out" is the general rule. This rule is not a good one to follow in therapy. In good therapy, everything has significance, but it takes experience to know what to do about it.

Where sexual abuse is concerned, the cues may look very fragmented to the uneducated eye, but the important thing is to notice the cue, acknowledge that it may be a statement of fact, encourage the Inner Children to speak freely, and stay receptive while waiting for the Inner Child to send the next clue. For example, if a person reports that an Inner Child is saying, "I was raped," as in one case, we repeat the statement and invite the Inner Child to give more information; "Your Inner Child says she was raped. What does she remember? Tell her it's safe now to tell the truth. Tell her you will never allow anything like that ever again." If no more information follows right away, the Inner Child may simply be waiting to see what the Grownup will do with the piece already given. Once reassured that we're concerned and on her side, the Inner Child invariably gives more information.

Sometimes acknowledging the clues as legitimate may be quite difficult, especially if what we know of a client's history seems to conflict with what the Inner Children are reporting. However, we can't stress enough the importance of taking these cues seriously. Our willingness to honor what they tell us invariably produces significant shifts in a person's life.

3. *The person tells the truth in our presence and is believed.* An Inner Child revealing a long-hidden secret of sexual abuse often bypasses the Grownup completely and temporarily takes over the personality. In other words, rather than report to the Grownup who then reports to us, the Inner Child will be pouring out such a flood of emotional energy that the Grownup can only stand aside and be a witness.

When this happens, the person we see revealing the secret is someone who though physically the person of today, is in all other respects, the young Inner Child, perhaps 2 or 3 years old, who is revealing the secret. Normal children that age don't lie about sexual abuse. If they're too young, shy, ashamed, afraid, or angry to speak clearly, their words may not tell us, but their bodies will. We may see it in clenched fists, whites of the eyes showing, or in the position the child was forced to assume when the abuse took place.

We are very careful to provide time and a place for sleep directly after sessions in which these memories have been revealed, because clients can experience a delayed reaction hours or even days later. Originally these abuses caused huge shock to the child's whole system, and recalling the abuses after so many years of suppression brings up what could be called an emotional after-shock. Bed rest and a full day off the next day or two aren't out of order. We also make sure one of us is available by phone for several days afterward.

4. *The Inner Child hears our honest reaction to the abuse.* Although we're committed to judging behavior, not people, we are human beings and there are times we need to react to the accounts we hear of sexual abuse. What we do is call time out and say we just need a few minutes to discharge our feelings and then we'll return to the Inner Child's process. We may say things like, "It's lucky for that man he's not alive today, because what I would like to do is kill him!" "I'm so sorry I wasn't there to stop this." This communicates three important thoughts: First, we totally accept the Inner Child's behavior as OK. Second, we are outraged that the Inner Child had to endure such treatment. And finally, we feel compassion for the burden of fear and shame the Inner Child has carried for so long.

5. *We give factual information to the Grownup and the Inner Child.* In contrast to the emotional message conveyed to the person in the preceding step, the information given in this step is factual. It includes what the Grownup needs to know to reassure the Inner Children:

— What you experienced *was* sexual abuse.

— That is a crime, because it's terribly harmful to children.

— Controlling sexual behavior between an adult and a child is the adult's responsibility; you were *never* responsible for what happened to you or for taking care of the abuser in any way.

— Your sexual feelings are safe and good, and no one has the right to tell you how, when, or where to have sex. If you experienced any physical pleasure, that's simply because the body is built for that. Liking a part of how it felt doesn't make you bad or responsible for what the abuser did.

6. *The client expresses rage at the abuse until finished doing so.* It's very important to allow the Inner Child to finish the raging. A tendency people have is to interrupt the anger so as to move on to forgiveness. We don't do it, and we don't let the Grownup do it. We let the Inner Child be the one to decide when she's through being angry.

7. *The Grownup, when ready, shares the secret with all persons potentially affected, past, present, or future.* Once the Grownup is clear about the nature and consequences of the abuse and has taken charge of the Inner Child in the matter of abuse, the information about what happened needs to be shared. Among those to be informed are all family members, especially those who might also have been abused, and anyone else directly affected by the abuser in any way, whether in the family or outside. If the abuser is still alive, parents of any children who might be at risk must be warned.

Just how or when the abuser is confronted must be the considered choice of the person's Grownup and the Co-therapist, in consultation with the Inner Children. Not that the Inner Children should have final say, but they need to understand they are entirely safe from any danger. We also recommend consulting a qualified professional, who will know the legal and psychological ramifications of such a confrontation. Just before this book went to press, we learned of some cases in which abusers arranged monetary settlements with their victims to cover the cost of therapy.

Revealing facts about the abuse is absolutely crucial for two reasons:

a. *The person who knowingly withholds such information must share responsibility for any abuse of the younger generation.* Child sexual abuse is an addiction that tends to grow worse over time rather than diminish. An abuser who does not get treatment will likely repeat and escalate his or her crime.

  b. *Until the secrets are revealed, full healing cannot take place*, because the Inner Child knows that the Grownup will protect the abuser first. It's very important for the Grownup to see that its first obligation is to the Inner Children, not to the abuser, and to allow the abuser to face the consequences of his or her actions.

8. *The person mourns the loss of childhood innocence—until finished doing so.* As with the rage, it is the Inner Children who need to cry, and they who will know when their crying is finished. At that point, they can reclaim their purity and innocence as a healing gift.

9. *The Abuser is separated completely from the Inner Child.* This separation must take place on at least two levels:

  a. *Behavioral level.* Until healing takes place, abused Inner Children remain trapped in their Family Spell filmstrip, trying desperately to protect themselves from the situation of many years ago. This means that when the Family Spell is activated in the here and now, the Inner Children will take over and employ inappropriate behavior, e.g., they may use compliant behavior, particularly with exploitive people, in an attempt to placate the abuser. Other Inner Children may use hostile, angry behavior to keep any potential abuser at a distance.

  Some Inner Children try to "save" the abuser—in social work with pedephiles, for example, or by praying for the abuser. If the person is a devout Catholic, for example, who believes "You should pray for those who hurt you," we suggest someone *else* to take over praying for the person. It's too much of a burden for a Inner Child. If the abuser is still alive and decides to go into treatment, all well and good, but neither the Grownup nor the Inner Child can control that, and it's important to stop trying to do so. Child sexual abuse is one of the most difficult addictions to break, and many abusers have insufficient will to do so.

  b. *Emotional level:* When the effects of child sexual abuse are healed completely, the person has reclaimed his or her own power, released the rage at the abuser, and chosen to forgive all who were responsible.

  Forgiving the abuser, the last step, is usually the most difficult. Not everyone takes that step, and for those who do, it's often, as Miriam says in her personal account at this end of this chapter, a grace. To support clients in claiming that grace for themselves, we give them information on forgiveness, and remain available to support whatever decision they make.

The preceding steps are relevant to all victims of child sexual abuse. The following section also concerns victims, but only those who have themselves become child sexual abusers.

Invitation to Healing for Child Sexual Abusers

We cannot hope to break the cycle of child sexual abuse until abusing adults discover the will and the way to heal. A single abuser can harm many children.

If you are or have been sexually abusing children, here is what we want to say to you.

1. *Every human being deserves the chance to heal deep wounds.* You too are a human being, and the pain, fear, rage, and sorrow that drive you to molest children is a source of suffering to you. You, no less than any other victims, have a right to healing.

2. *You can unburden yourself of this terrible secret,* **and** you need to understand the law regarding mandated reporting. It varies from state to state, but what it boils down to is that any professional who suspects that a child is being sexually abused must report to the authorities or be civilly liable. The only professionals exempted from this requirement are Catholic or Episcopal priests operating in the Sacrament of Confession. Therefore, no one can tell you how much you will or will not divulge: Simply know that if you do divulge enough information for a professional to identify the child, you leave them no choice under the law but to report you to the authorities.

3. *If you are committed to healing, we believe one of the fastest methods may be Inner Family Healing.* If our theory holds true, then you have at least one Inner Child in the driver's seat, unable to connect with the present and too young to manage an adult life, who is sexually abusing children in the mistaken belief that it is the best way available to avoid being victimized in a situation he or she survived a long time ago.

The fact that the impulse to abuse children sexually comes from one or more Inner Children does not in any way relieve you of responsibility for the consequences of actions taken under such Inner Children's influence.

If you, in an adult body, molest children, you, the whole person, are responsible for committing a deeply destructive crime against another human being being. Nothing will change that. It doesn't matter that an Inner Child was in charge. It doesn't matter if the Inner Grownup didn't know. The Grownup is still responsible. The good news is that accepting that responsibility is the beginning of hope and healing.

Once the Inner Grownup chooses to accept responsibility, Inner Family healing can make a great difference to you. Understanding that Inner Children are running this part of your show opens the way for your Inner Grownup to locate these Children, to ask them why they feel the need to sexually abuse other children, and to meet their needs another way.

4. You can take the first step on the road to healing by doing the following:

  a. *Recognize that child sexual abuse is an addiction just as powerful as alcoholism or drugs.* Fortunately, we know something about addiction through various programs that have been success- ful—Alcoholics Anonymous, Alanon, and the myriad other groups that are utilizing the same basic wisdom. Therefore, some of the same wisdom that has enabled AA to heal so many also applies to you: You cannot do it alone. You need to trust a higher power. You can do it only one day at a time. If no other sources of support are available, join an AA group. It's a cleans- ing, strengthening process—not the whole answer, but an im- portant resource.

  b. *Stop sexually abusing children.* As long as you are actively engag- ing in the addictive behavior, you are not only breaking the law and thus jeopardizing your own well-being and that of others, but your Inner Children are in charge and so is your system of denial. Working with an active addict is pointless. If you find yourself unwilling to quit, but know you need to, pray for willingness—"God, You know I'm not willing, but I'm willing to be made willing"—and then get help.

  c. *Make the commitment to find and heal your Inner Children.* Read this book several times, paying special attention to chapters 7, 8, and 9. Begin asking these Inner Children what goes on with them when the urge to sexually abuse begins. When you hear their answers, write them down and believe them.

We have committed ourselves to a breakthrough in the healing of child sexual abusers. We are in the early stages, but by Fall of 1991, we will have trained some professionals in this method. We invite your support in this effort, especially if you are someone who has sexually molested children and want to heal yourself. We expect to collect more data and case examples on abusers. For now, however, the following "personal accounts" include only non-abusing victims of child sexual abuse. They show how Inner Family work produced freedom, healing, and forgiveness for them.

Two Personal Accounts

In the following accounts, we have changed the names and some of the details of the events, because although "Miriam" and "Helga" have resolved the issues for themselves, they've chosen to respect their families' reticence with respect to these events.

Helga

You met Helga in chapter 6. She is the gifted teacher with occasional lapses, but whose Grownup skills are impressive. You will see from the following that she has overcome a great deal of childhood abuse to become who she is today.

> I had been doing therapy with Jacqui for a short time and making progress. I was learning to protect myself when someone became abusive, even subtly so. Here's an example of how I'd learned to handle that.
>
> On one occasion, which I thought was going to be very non-threatening (so my defenses were completely down), a revelation occurred to me regarding little Julie. It happened in a group of people who I had always experienced as open and accepting. This day, each member in the group had shared an incident of healing in the recent past, and now it was my turn. I told the others how I had been taught to get in touch with my Inner Child and that a healing of the lack of nurturing and good parenting in my childhood was taking place inside me. Two individuals in the group gave very strong negative reactions to this method of healing and tried to invalidate my experience by their statements and questions. The more they questioned, the more defensive I became. And as I spoke, the very symptoms that had brought me into this conversation on healing began to recur. Little Julie was afraid and threatened. As soon as I realized this, I graciously removed myself

from the situation and found a quiet place to soothe Little Julie. As I did, I became acutely aware that Julie's greatest fear was the fear of rejection, and I had unwittingly placed her in that situation. On this and several other occasions, as I gained insights into the fear-to-nurturing sequence, the healing process seemed to progress in leaps and bounds.

My emotional life progressed fairly smoothly for a while, then unexpectedly, I became very sad, almost depressed, and was aware that I didn't feel at all good about myself. I wasn't having a stomach ache or anxiety, so I couldn't understand what was happening. However, my heart was very heavy. I contacted Jacqui, and in her supportive, accepting interaction with me, she enabled me to relate to her an incident of sexual abuse I had experienced when I was 12 or 13 years old.

Like most 12-year-old girls, I was very self-conscious about my body and its impending and visible physical maturity. I also felt nervous and tense in the presence of my mother, who would enforce harsh words and commands with blows from her hand or the green tree branch switch she kept on top of the refrigerator. So conditioned was I after a while that she didn't even need to abuse me to induce my terror and compliance.

Usually her demands were simply abusive, but this time she had more in mind. I won't go into the details here—not because I'm ashamed of her behavior, but because I have no wish to magnify it by repeating it.

The point is that at the time I felt entirely helpless to resist her demands, and after I'd done what she asked, I felt dirty, shameful, loathsome, and violated. It must have seemed like an eternity when it happened, but at some point in the incident, I shut off all feeling and all memory of it. Even when the experience resurfaced in my consciousness many years later, most details still eluded me, but the piercing gaze of my mother and the feeling that I was filthy and worthless were as vivid as the day they occurred.

Unearthing this incident revealed another Inner Child, located in my heart. She had been unable to receive love for herself. For after all, how can she accept love if she considered herself filthy and worthless? This new Child, Gloria, is older than Julie and has experienced a trauma different from Julie's. Julie feels rejected by others, whereas Gloria rejects herself, feels pain in her heart, and experiences shame towards herself. She obviously needed nurturing and counter-parenting in those areas. And she has since received them and continues to do so.

Miriam

"Miriam" was the first person to teach us about using Inner Family healing to treat the wounds of sexual abuse. Her trust in us enabled us to accompany her on the healing journey, and in fact, much of this chapter is based on thinking in which she was a major collaborator.

Miriam taught us how deeply sexual abuse injures a person and how important it is for the person's Grownup to acknowledge and accept that this deep injury occurred. Complete healing is possible, but we cannot dictate the timetable for it. What survivors of abuse must do in the interim, as Miriam has done, is to decide, regardless of the injury, to live a full life.

Miriam is a very beautiful young woman with classic facial bone structure, elegant hands, and a lovely, strong body. In addition to her physical beauty, she is genuinely kind and profoundly spiritual. She also, when we first met, had a nervous laugh, and sometimes the whites of her eyes would show as if she were afraid, like a young horse that has been brutalized physically.

Miriam came primarily at first to talk about a relationship with a young man she was dating. Over the next few months, it became clear that this relationship was emotionally abusive. Moreover, Miriam and her boyfriend couldn't have been much further apart spiritually and culturally. He was a devout Moslem, she a devout Catholic. He was a product of Middle Eastern culture, where women were little better than chattel. She was a brilliant American and very much of a feminist. When faced with these facts, Miriam decided to end the relationship.

The sessions were winding down and she seemed to be doing fine, when Miriam attended a workshop where she was teamed up with two people. One of them, it turned out, had been a sexual abuser. Although on the surface, nothing happened, yet the way this person was using his hands triggered a deep reaction in Miriam. We believed then—and now know—that Miriam was reacting from actual childhood memories.

We invited Miriam to act as co-therapist, which was a way of assuring her a greater sense of control in the sessions and also of giving her a means of conveying information to help us when we were stuck. Her ability as Co-therapist contributed enormously to our ability to help her.

The healing began in earnest when Miriam's three-year-old revealed the secret by showing clearly in a physical way how she was sodomized. As a result of telling the story and releasing her feelings of shame, self-loathing, and horror, the three-year-old became wonderfully free and delightfully happy, regaining and reclaiming her innocence.

The five-year-old, however, was very angry. It was she who stopped the sexual abuse by avoiding the abuser. We began with her by congratulating her on stopping the sexual abuse and not allowing it. Then later we discovered the five-year-old's determination to get revenge. It took quite a while to get the five-year-old to understand that revenge was very destructive to all Miriam's Inner Children, especially one, who was very frightened and agitated by the five-year-old's anger.

Part of the difficulty in letting go of the anger was that, as a devout Catholic, Miriam felt constrained to pray for her abuser, which outraged the five-year-old. After the abuse had come out in the open, we made sure she knew she didn't have to pray for her uncle (the abuser). Others, we told her, would pray for him and we arranged for that. It is crucial to honor the individual's belief system.

Although the abuse ceased when she was five and Miriam had suppressed the memories, she continued to make other decisions that built on top of the original foundation of sexual abuse. For example, her nine-year-old learned to be a caretaker, a little compliant mother. She assumed responsibility for her younger sister Annie, whom she considered to be her baby, someone she could have for herself to love. When Miriam's mother had an illness, however, and the baby sister was taken to live with an aunt, Miriam's nine-year-old felt betrayed and made the decision not to love or trust anyone. This also had to be spoken about and dealt with before there could be healing.

Here's Miriam's story in her own words.

I have five Inner Children: their ages are about 8 months, three years, five years, nine years, and twelve years, respectively.

When I first started therapy with Mary, nothing much seemed to happen. We talked about things I was having trouble with currently. In particular, I was dating a guy who wasn't very nice to me—I didn't even like him, really, but I was addicted to him. When I look at it now, I realize my Inner Children had picked someone who was abusive like my uncle.

Then one week I had a rebirthing session: that's when you breathe connected breaths (no pauses). I did a lot of crying in that session about there not having been enough love for me when I was little. It was after the rebirthing that my Inner Baby came up. Her name is Susan. She's the only one with a name.

I think that for quite a while after that, I was building trust with Mary. A couple of my Inner Children came up. One, my three-year-old, is in my stomach/diaphragm area. I love my three-year-old. She's just great!

And then there is my nine-year-old. Nine was the year when I had a problem with a particular schoolteacher, but the whole issue was really a continuation of dealing with my mother and the abuse.

While this work was going on, the thought kept going through my head, "I was sodomized." I didn't tell Mary those particular words. What I said was "These words go through my head, saying I was abused." I couldn't remember anything that happened. But since the way I put it didn't provide her with any new information, we didn't do anything with it. At the time, neither of us seemed to think that it amounted to anything.

At that point we were getting ready to stop the therapy and I went on vacation. When I came back, Mary said I was stifling my masculine energy, and we should do some work with that. We did one session in which nothing came up. But during the next week, I felt very nervous, and my arms felt so weak and this memory of my uncle and me kept coming up. I was on a swing, and he was talking to me and I was feeling very very angry, thinking 'he shouldn't be talking to me.' But I kept thinking, 'That's silly. He isn't saying anything bad.'

The next session with Mary, we worked with the feelings in my arms. She kept saying "Your arms are *strong! Feel* the strength!" and I was hitting a pillow to experience that strength but not feeling strong at all. In fact, I was becoming more and more frightened. Mary then had me move from the floor onto the couch. I had this sense of my wrists being constrained. I began to relive the physical experience of being abused sexually—it was really strange. I was crying, screaming, trying to get away from someone, and, at the same time, I was watching myself go through all these motions, thinking "how could I not connect with these emotions?" I didn't remember what was going on.

For the next three to five sessions, we just kept working on these physical memories, except my three-year-old started talking about it, telling exactly what my uncle did. Most of what I said then I've since forgotten, because I've been healed of it. I felt responsible for what happened and was angry at myself for that. I believed the lies he told me and found it difficult to accept the truth. I was angry at my parents because I thought they knew. I remember carrying on when it was time to go to my grandmother's, and they made me go with them anyway. I was angry that God knew and He didn't stop him. I remembered the places that weren't safe—the bathroom wasn't safe, because he'd come in there. And my grandparents' room wasn't safe. I've always had a dislike for the Infant (Jesus) of Prague, and, when I was working in therapy with Mary, I remembered my uncle abusing me in my grandparents' room where this statue was. I remember looking at the statue and thinking in my distress, Why aren't You helping me?

Another Child came up right after the three-year-old began to tell everything. It was my five-year-old, and she was very angry at my uncle, but even more enraged at the three-year-old for having told Mary and for letting it happen in the first place. What she didn't realize was that she was really perpetuating the abuse that my uncle had done. It took a few sessions to get her to realize that.

Letting go of the rage at my uncle was a grace. One key was choosing, in my Grownup self, to forgive even though I didn't feel like doing that at all. Another key was telling my family the truth and discovering that my uncle had lied about my parents knowing and consenting to it all. My Inner Children had actually been afraid that my family knew about the abuse and somehow sanctioned it. I think my Children were also afraid that "he" would punish us for telling—even though he's been dead for years.

Now that I have been freed from the deep pain of being sexually abused, I can see how all along there were these two children in me (three and five) acting out the abuse both internally and externally. As I become more and more aware of these old patterns, I stop them, give the Children permission to say no, to relax, to feel innocent, and I'm not struggling with anger the way I used to.

❖

Child sexual abuse is one of the most profound traumas a person can undergo. There are those who say that it's impossible to deal fully with other issues until the sexual abuses have been unearthed. Others believe its effects can never be healed completely.

While this has not been our experience, we do recognize that forgiving sexual abuse is, at best, easier said than done. We also have seen that the forgiveness process is facilitated—even made possible—by resorting to spiritual means. This is part of what is described in the chapter on forgiveness, next.

9

Forgiving

An Act of Self-Esteem

For some of us, going to the moon looks easier than forgiving some of the people who have wronged us, especially when they did so very early in our lives before we could defend ourselves. Nevertheless, no matter what has taken place in the past, forgiveness is one of the best bargains on the planet, because the alternative—chronic anger—exacts from us a high price physically, mentally, emotionally, and spiritually.

In reading this, one might think we're saying anger is bad, but we aren't saying that at all. In fact, anger is like all the emotions in that it serves a positive purpose. Just for starters, it gives us energy to fight when we're threatened and staying power when we need to be determined. The issue is not whether anger is good or bad, it's whether we use it to further our well-being or to trap ourselves in the past.

One of the chief reasons forgiving is so difficult is that so few of us truly understand the nature and meaning of forgiveness. Rather, we labor under a whole pile of misconceptions. In this chapter, we intend to empower you to embrace forgiveness as a way of life at every level—not in a mealy-mouthed way, but as a way of embracing life itself and ourselves living it: Accordingly, we begin by sweeping away misconceptions about what forgiveness means. We then go on to define forgiveness (to the extent that it's definable), explain how to create a vision of forgiveness, and describe a variety of techniques to exercise our powers of forgiveness.

Myths About Forgiveness

As a society, we know very little about forgiveness. Rather than free ourselves to forgive, we stand paralyzed by the following myths:

- *If I forgive someone but don't feel it, then I'm being a phony.*

  Making the decision to forgive isn't a feeling. It's an act of will, a proclamation. That means the decision can be made based on nothing more than common sense about the alternatives.

- *If I give up my anger, I'll be helpless and defenseless.*

  Hardly. This is the voice of an Inner Child who has assigned to anger the magical power to keep harm at a distance by frightening people away, and who fears that forgiving means totally forfeiting any right to use anger in self-defense. In actual fact, chronic anger erodes our defenses, because some people have trouble thinking clearly and creatively about alternatives when they're angry.

- *Some people don't deserve to be forgiven.*

  Deserving to be forgiven isn't the issue. Of course, if someone has wronged us and is willing to make up for it, that's wonderful. But whether they do or not, the one who pays the price for our own unforgiveness is us, not the other person. Our holding anger against them simply perpetuates their power to hurt us.

- *Forgiving someone just gives them the idea they can go out and do it again.*

  The person may choose to go out and do it again, but that has nothing to do with forgiving. Forgiveness in and of itself is for the forgiver, not for the forgiven. For the unrepentant, being forgiven is a burden.

- *Forgiving and asking forgiveness are weak.*

  In our experience, it takes great strength to overcome one's pride (pride being the first line of resistance to reconciliation). The apology that comes from weakness or fear has nothing to do with forgiving or asking forgiveness. True forgiveness comes out of a commitment to freedom and self-esteem—a desire to affirm and strengthen the best in oneself for the long haul.

- *Asking forgiveness means saying "I'm wrong and you were right."*

Not so. Forgiveness has nothing to do with right and wrong. You can ask forgiveness if the other person was wrong and you were right or vice versa, or if you were both right or both wrong. The only reason forgiveness is needed is that someone is holding onto anger or hurt. Asking for forgiveness means asking the person to give up staying angry, then relinquishing the "right" to punish or act vengefully. It dissolves unhealthy bonding between you and the other person. That's all.

- *Asking forgiveness means "I lose."*

   Not unless being right matters more to you than being truly at peace. Most unforgiveness accompanies a desire to define another person as the bad guy and thus exonerate ourselves from any responsibility or blame. Forgiveness cleans the slate so that both people can get right, both people can "win." That's not possible where vengeance remains an option.

- *If I forgive, that means I'll have to trust the person.*

   Not true: Forgiving means being free of the bondage of anger. Trusting is expecting someone to behave in a certain way because they say they will or represent themselves as that kind of person. Trust is something that, once lost, must be *earned back*.

- *People who really love each other don't have to ask forgiveness.*

   Whoever wrote "Love is never having to say you're sorry" was either naive or temporarily insane. Who is in a better position to wound—knowingly or unknowingly—than the person to whom we have opened our heart most deeply? How could we possibly live and work together without letting one another know that we regret insensitivities and petty self-indulgences, not to mention major betrayals?

So if all these are myths about forgiveness, what's the real story?

Forgiveness Defined

Webster's Dictionary defines "forgive" as follows:

1. To give up resentment against or the desire to punish; to stop being angry with; to pardon.
2. To give up all claim to punish or exact penalty for (an offense); to overlook.

3. To cancel or remit, as a debt, fine, or penalty
   Synonym—pardon, absolve, remit, cancel, release

These sound fine, as far as they go, but if we meditate on the forgive-ness process within ourselves, we find that we actually do not know precisely what forgiveness is. We don't *know* what enables holocaust victims to forgive their captors. We don't *know* how people who are sexually abused forgive their abusers. We don't even know how people forgive themselves. It is truly a mystery: the more deeply we delve into the subject and the experience, the more levels, subtleties, and possibil-ities we find it contains.

But this much we can say about forgiveness:

- It arises out of an initial commitment to be at peace with oneself and others.
- It involves letting go of a fixed negative attitude toward some-one.
- It benefits the person who does the forgiving more than the person being forgiven.
- It's an expression of self-esteem.

Expressed in the context of healing the Inner Family, we forgive a person when our Inner Children:

1. Stop using anger against self or other as a magical way of controlling the past, present, and future
2. Stop fueling anger by accepting the past instead of arguing against it as being good or bad, fair or unfair
3. Look to our own Grownup instead of to the person we're angry at to give us what we lacked as children
4. Surrender authority to the Grownup regarding what to do about what happened or didn't happen
5. Know they can safely have all their feelings and thoughts about that person, knowing that the Grownup will limit their actions to what conforms with their long-term well-being.

But how does one get to this point? If we don't even know what forgiveness is, how do we get our stubborn, proud, wounded selves to make it happen?

Fortunately, we don't have to know precisely *how* to forgive or even *what* forgiveness is in order to take the first step toward doing so: developing a vision.

A Vision of Forgiveness

When President Kennedy declared we would go to the moon in 10 years, NASA personnel gagged. They knew it was not technically feasible, and so did he. But he had the vision, and that was enough to enable him to take the first step, making the commitment anyway. NASA beat his deadline. We can do the same.

However, in the beginning, we may react just like the NASA personnel who gagged because they knew the technology didn't exist. For some of us, deep and long-standing resentments, especially toward someone with whom we've been close, have so permeated the fabric of our lives that we can't begin to imagine what it would be like to have forgiven the person. In such instances, it's easier to say what we *don't* want than what we *do* want. What we *don't* want are the experiences of *un*forgiveness:

1. *Black-and-white thinking:* an inability to remember or to feel good about the worthy things a person is or has done, combined with judgmental thoughts about how they don't measure up

2. *Cutting off:* unfeeling indifference to someone with whom we've been close

3. *Overattachment:* inability to remain emotionally unaffected by any action the person may take; taking every move personally

4. *Rage, and wanting to hurt:* wanting to kick someone in the teeth, thoughts of physical revenge, murder

5. *Repulsion:* inability to accept the person's existence, wanting the person to disappear completely from the earth

6. *Resistance to continued obligation:* inability to care for the person's needs without resentment

7. *Envy:* resentment of any good fortune that befalls the person

8. *Powerlessness:* a sense of being mentally, physically, and emotionally smaller or weaker than the person who hurt us

9. *Self-pity:* inability to see past one's own pain to appreciate another's or to see humor in the situation

10. *Guilt and shame:* self-loathing for feeling negative toward the

person or for being the kind of person that someone would want to hurt like that.

What a recipe for misery! Nobody in their right mind would want to stay in that kind of experience for very long, right? especially when they can have the opposite:

1. *Connectedness*, openness with oneself and the other
2. *Understanding* that someone who hurts us can also love us
3. *Clear individuation*, knowing viscerally that another person's action defines who they are, not who we are
4. *Peace*, thoughts of goodwill
5. *Intimacy*, the freedom to choose to be close or distant with that person
6. *Open-heartedness*, the ability to serve the person without resentment
7. *Gratitude and generosity* of spirit, pleasure in someone else's good fortune
8. *Equality*, a sense of being physically the same size as the person who hurt us, also equal in other ways
9. *Lightness*, release from self-pity; wisdom from the experience; eventually the ability to feel light or even laugh at what happened and what we made of it
10. *Self acceptance*, affection for ourselves, compassion for our pain.

So this is what things look and feel like when one successfully shoots for the moon regarding forgiveness. To begin creating a vision that has power for yourself, try this next exercise.

First, select someone who you are committed to forgiving.

Now, imagine that you are very old. Many of your friends have already passed on.

You are walking through a park in the springtime. The breeze is gentle and the birds are singing their hearts out. Daffodils are at their peak and, with the warming sun, the flowering trees are suddenly blooming.

Looking back over your long life, you are aware of having lived fully and well. The pains and the joys have woven a rich tapestry for you, and you have gained wisdom, humor, and a measure of peacefulness. Life seems long and short at the same time, long because so much has happened, and short because you know there's not much time remaining. So you savour this spring day, feeling grateful for every detail of beauty you see as you walk along.

You notice, to the side, sunlight falling on a little curved bench, inviting you to come and sit a while to enjoy the view. The dappled sunlight, falling through the trees, speckles the forest with gold and then washes rippling over a meadow and spreads out to a large lake. As you approach the bench, you see someone coming down the path from the other direction. This is the person you chose at the beginning of this journey.

You haven't seen one another for years and years. And then the memory comes back of what happened long ago, and how it was allowed to stand between you for such a long time. You both stop, remembering. And you both see one another as you are this spring day, at the end of your lives.

Around you both is a beautiful light, like a mist of gentle affection in which you rest, looking, at yourself and this person.

You know you're being given a chance, perhaps for the last time in this life, to heal the old wounds. The other person knows also. What will you do?

You both move to the bench, sit down, and look out over the lake to the meadow. After some moments of silence, the words come to your mind, "Will you love as you have been loved? . . . the moment has come, and you turn to one another and speak from your heart.

If the person you've selected has passed on already, or even if they're alive, it might be useful to write him or her a letter to express what's in your heart. Whether you send it or not is not important.

The predominant experiences of forgiveness are freedom and strength and, as we said at the beginning of the chapter, it's one of the best bargains around, no matter what it takes.

Some Processes for Forgiving

There doesn't seem to be any set or right way to experience the process of forgiving someone. It's very personal. For one of us, it may be simply a matter of declaring it, and it's done. For another, it's a matter of time healing the wound, and one day we wake up and find we'd like to see the person again. For still another, it's a constant sore that doesn't go away, no matter how much therapy, how much crying, how much raging we do, and then suddenly we realize that what's in the way is our own guilt, which we've been projecting onto the other person; once we see our own self-condemnation, we're free.

More often than not, unforgiveness has something to do with our Family Spell, an old memory picture that has laid itself over the present scene, rendering us temporarily incapable of being in the here-and-now. In such cases, we actually need to work with the early memory rather than the person in the here-and-now.

We're going to suggest some ways to go about forgiving that have been helpful to us and others. The basic strategies involve one or more of the following: expressing feelings that have been denied or suppressed, identifying and relieving any fears the Inner Children may have, revealing the Family Spell images that may be in the way, and, finally, surrendering pride. As preparation for any of the following exercises, imagine yourself facing the person you have committed to forgiving.

Write a Letter

One of the simplest forgiveness processes, if not the shortest, is to write the person a letter (which you do not plan to send). The purpose of writing the letter is to help you establish a new, clear basis for continued relationship with that person. It doesn't matter if the person is living or not.

The letter should express how you feel and why, reveal what you haven't communicated, make a request for what you want, and announce that you now forgive the person.

You have completed the exercise only when you can say the letter is authentic *and* you would welcome receiving such a letter yourself. Don't be surprised if it takes several drafts to get to that point. Then and only then, decide whether or not to send the letter.

If I Could Get My Hands On . . .!

This exercise provides a way to express and let go of all the murderous fantasies you might consciously or unconsciously be nursing. Here's how it goes:

Picture miniature versions of yourself and the other person about a foot high and four to six feet in front of you. Get clear that this tiny version of you is absolutely safe.

Now, let the image of yourself express all your feelings *fully*. If you want to blow the person up, dismember them, let this image go through those motions. It can be as awful as you want.

Direct any anger *outward*. Under no circumstances should you allow this image to turn on itself, you, or any of your Inner Children. That's merely a way to avoid expressing anger at a person toward whom it feels dangerous to be angry. If that's what this image wants to do, say no, and keep inviting it to express the real resentment outwardly.

Whenever the image stops being angry, ask, "How do you feel? Do you want to do more? Keep going until you're finished." When the image has finished, ask what it wants now—a hug, a rest, a puppy.

Check out all the Inner Children to see if they also want to express anger or other feelings toward the person who hurt them.

I Could Just Scream

Taught for years by many therapeutic notables,* screaming is excellent for those of us who are angry at someone but not entirely sure why. The purpose of the exercise is to discharge excess emotional energy so that buried thinking and perceptions can rise to conscious awareness. The drawbacks are that you may get a sore throat and it's very noisy. You'll need a place where you can make a huge racket without being disturbed (if necessary you can scream into a pillow). It helps sometimes to beat a bed with a tennis racket at the same time. If all else fails, take a car, making sure *all* the windows are rolled up, and go park somewhere along a parkway. You can do it alone, or, better still, have a friend come along.

At full voice, scream the first angry thought that comes to mind about the person. Then the next thought and the next. But don't get lost in thinking. If you only have one thought, just keep screaming that over and over. Eventually, once you have the predominant thought, you don't even need to scream the words. Let the words go and just make sounds, making sure the sound rises like a roar from your belly, not your throat.

When the feelings come up, don't worry about what they are or why you feel them. Long-standing resentments almost always include pain and fear,

---

* Notables who have promoted screaming: Dan Casriel, founder of Daytop and of the New Identity Process, Janov of Primal Scream Therapy, Alexander Lowen of Bioenergetics, Fritz Perls who developed Gestalt therapy.

broken dreams, and often humiliation. Your purpose is not to sort through the garbage to label it, but to flush it out of the system.

Express all the feelings until finished. Then hold your Inner Children and allow the love to flow toward them.

The Inner Children may resist expressing their rage, for example, because "It won't do any good." It's true that it won't change the past, and it's important to know that expressing feelings, especially rage, does not change anything outside ourselves. But that's not the purpose of expressing feelings.

The purpose of expressing feelings authentically is to enable us to discharge them and make way for feeling good in the present. The reason screaming helps is that it releases the dam of resentment that actually keeps the lid on feeling hopeless, helpless, and despairing. As long as the lid stays on, we're stuck with the despair. But if we can blow the lid off and experience the despair, we can let it go to make way for something else. And that, of course is what we're after. Who cares about past injury to us if we feel good and valuable in the present?

If expressing feelings doesn't provide any relief, then one of two things is likely: (1) the feelings being expressed are substitutes for the real feelings (e.g., we may be expressing anger but really feeling sadness underneath), and we need to get to the real feelings before we can discharge; or (2) we're using the feelings as a way to make another person change ("If I stay sad—or angry or scared—for long enough, you'll have to do what I want (take care of me, stop hurting me, come back, feel guilty).

If neither of these two exercises does the trick, then we help people examine more deeply the origins of their resistance to forgiving.

When Was the First Time You Felt This Way?

When the Family Spell has been activated, it's likely that the feelings and thoughts that keep us stuck are depicted on the filmstrip, and we need to forgive what happened in that original scene before the present-day impasse will start to ease.

So have your Grownup ask the Children when was the last time they felt this way about someone. An Inner Child will remind you, and the scene or memory will come to mind. Don't worry if the response doesn't seem strictly logical at this point. The first memory that comes up may be just a bridge to the one you're looking for. You may cycle back through several such scenes before you get to the original one.

When the memory comes up, have the Grownup tell the Inner Children that they are perfectly safe, that the Grownup is in charge and will allow no harm whatsoever to come to them. Say that you love them, and you're not leaving them under any circumstances whatsoever. If you're aware of a lot of anxiety, you might want to call or ask someone to come over and simply be present with you while you explore the memories. Once the Inner Children are reassured, proceed by asking them these questions:

1. "What do you remember happening?"
2. "How did you feel?"
3. "What did you decide?"
4. "What do you think that did for you then?"
5. "What do you think that's doing for you now?" for the other Inner Children? for people you love?
6. "What could life be like if that decision didn't run your life?"
7. What would it be worth to you to have your life be like that?
8. What are you willing to change?

If I Forgive, Then . . .

Here's another way to get at what the Inner Children fear will happen if they forgive someone. Complete, in writing, a series of statements, as in the following:

"If I forgive, then I'll have to . . ."
"If I forgive, then I won't be able to . . ."
"If I forgive, then the person will . . ."
"If I forgive, then you'll . . ."
"If I forgive, then people will . . ."
"If I forgive, then life will never. . ."
"If I forgive, then no one will ever . . . "
"If I forgive, then . . .God will (or won't) . . ."
"If I forgive, then . . .I'll never . . . "
"If I forgive, then . . .Mom or Dad will (or won't) . . ."
"If I forgive, then . . .I'll always

Keep going until you have several phrases that evoke some emotional response. Then go back to the list and read each one aloud, asking, "and then? and then? to see what the chain of reasoning is.

Here's an example:

If I forgive my mother, then she won't feel guilty any more
           And then?   she'll go away

And then?   I'll be alone.
And then?   I'll die.

So one of this person's Inner Children has it wired up that if he forgives his mother, he'll die. That's the thinking of a very young child and has no relevance in the here-and-now. The Grownup can speak with this Inner Child, reassure him that he will not die in the here-and-now because his Grownup is now his mother and his father. When the Inner Child has taken in that information, even partially, the Grownup moves on to any other statements that carried an emotional charge.

How Do I Do to *Myself* What This Person Did to Me?

Often, we are angry at someone else less for what they have done to us than for what we have done to ourselves. In some way or another, the other person has simply echoed or replicated our own self-abuse. This pattern is what is known as "projection." We project onto someone else the responsibility for what we ourselves are doing.

One way of looking at projection is to put it in terms of the filmstrip of the Family Spell: We have one Inner Child who is abusing another, and our Grownup doesn't know it until we can see the behavior in someone else by projecting the filmstrip image onto them. Then we fight that person, with the combined energy of the enraged Inner Victim striking back *and* the Inner Abuser who is happy to have someone else take the rap.

To flush the Inner Abuser out of hiding, we ask the question, How do I do to myself what I see this person doing to me? It's helpful to try a few different phrases, to see what rings for us. Some examples:

- A woman gets angry because someone has ignored her. She can ask herself, "How do I treat myself as if I weren't there? How do I treat myself as if I didn't count? How do I disregard my importance in a crowd?"

-     A man is angry at his boss for picking out only the negatives about a report that took two weeks to prepare. In the process of forgiving his boss, he might ask himself, "How do I discount the value of my work? How do I withhold positive feedback from myself? How do I pick on myself? How do I look for negatives instead of positives in myself and others?"

When the answer to the question becomes clear, one can ask both Inner

Children's forgiveness for allowing the abuse, promise to love and care for them both, and commit to preventing any such behavior from occurring either internally or externally from now on.

When All Else Fails . . . Forgive God and Pray

We're unsure how much forgiveness is consistently possible using strictly psychological means. Some resentments go so deep it feels as if we were born with them. Our pain, rage, and fear have permeated the very cells of our body, putting the decision to forgive well beyond the power of the intellect. Such deep unforgiveness may include a sense that God Himself made a mistake of which He disapproves and we're it. If our parents didn't even want us to be born, we may feel the universe itself is a chaos with only a thin layer of order stretched over it. The very ground beneath our feet is ready to betray our trust. These deep wounds tend to come from our earlier years. It's tough enough to forgive someone who hurts us when we are adults: In most cases, they couldn't have mistreated us without our cooperation. But what about cases where we weren't collaborators in our own abuse? What about the rejecting parent who never did want us? What about the abusing relative who hurt or molested us when we were too small to understand or defend ourselves. What about the society who has treated us as not even human? Most of us have a few bones to pick with God. After all, isn't it the Creator who allowed life to be so painful? What about the God who took our daddy when we needed him so much?

No mere act of will dislodges such deep trauma. In such cases, forgiveness needs to include forgiving the person(s) for hurting us, ourselves for being hurt, and God for allowing it. Sometimes even after years of work—therapy, self-control, and wishing—our resentment doesn't yield. Then what? If you're angry at God but have never told Him so, we recommend you do it. If suppressing your feelings is what's keeping you stuck, then expressing your feelings can be extremely healing. And God's big enough to take it. You don't need to protect Him from us, you, or anyone else.

If after expressing anger at God you find that you feel no different, you may be transferring onto Him the image of someone from your childhood, probably a parent. God the Father often looks like our own father or mother. Freudians have known this for a long time—"I never knew an atheist with a good relationship with his father" is one expression of that wisdom.

If chronic rage at God is your way of evading dealing with your own parents, we don't believe you can know whether you actually have any issues with God until you have started to deal with your own parents.

Ultimately, we believe the nature and source of forgiveness are spiritual, which opens up: (1) prayer, (2) healing of memories, and (3) spiritual practice.

Prayer.

Actually, the heading on this section is misleading. For us, prayer is the first recourse, not the last resort. We encourage people to begin their own conversation with God and to pray with us for the power to forgive. "Lord, I don't have what it takes. I'm doing my best, but if you want me to really love this person, you'll have to do it through me" is a prayer that God has often honored in the past. "I'm not willing, but I'm willing to be made willing."

Healing of Memories.

Healing of memories offers a way of dealing with profound unforgiveness. We ask God to present the memories that need to be healed, and then for Jesus to be there with us as we go back into the memory, to provide the protection and healing power we need for completing the forgiveness process.

Spiritual practice.

For people who were raised in the church but have drifted away, or for those who have a cordial relationship with Jesus, we recommend taking *communion* daily.

For others, we suggest setting aside some *meditation* time each day to do nothing but receive from God. No strings. Books on Centering Prayer are helpful in this practice.

These spiritual practices strengthen us through a connection that bypasses the intellect. That way our busy minds can't interfere with the healing. The same is true for our last recommendation, the practice of gratitude.

...and Practice Gratitude

Finally, we recommend the practice of *gratitude*. Giving thanks generates positive energy, and if you stick with it, asking for the power to make it real, it can produce miracles for you. We can speculate that the psalmist was being precise when he wrote, "God inhabits the praises of his people." If it feels phony to give thanks, we urge you to take a fake-it-till-you-make-it approach to expressing gratitude for as many things as you can possibly think of, including the incidents over which you are so upset.

This recommendation is confirmed by our experience and observation that crises and tragedies usually contain within them the seeds of release and healing. "No pain, no gain" is another way of expressing this truth. The pain is eased, however, when we consciously and deliberately choose to see the process as healing, which expressing gratitude helps us do. Choosing to see a painful process as healing is not to be confused with choosing masochism or martyrdom; we aren't recommending people deliberately put themselves into painful situations. Life itself presents us with enough difficulties without our seeking them out. When we suggest practicing gratitude, we're saying no more than, "Choose to stay attentive to the good." A recent book may be worth buying for the title alone, To believe it is to see it.

❖

In the final analysis, forgiving means learning to say "yes" to all that was, is, and will be, instead of "It shouldn't be that way." Forgiveness means choosing to open to all that is in life, including the painful, instead of only what leaves us feeling secure or pain-free. It means taking a leap of faith that in the end things will all work out, whether we would have preferred that they happen the way they did or not.

To say this another way, we will need to forgive not only ourselves and others, but life itself, and by implication, the Intelligence that is the Source of life.

Forgiveness, at last, means accepting that suffering is one of our best teachers, and that it is what we suffer that melts away the gristle of our self-centeredness and separation from our Inner Children and from our brothers and sisters out in the world.

10

Summary and Afterthoughts on Loving Ourselves

We began this book on Inner Family Healing as a vehicle for answering the call to love ourselves. You have now learned that one way to love yourself is to train your Grownup in loving and caring for your Inner Children, those wounded, courageous, intelligent, creative, independent, and sometimes exasperating parts of us that will never—and should never—get any older.

You've learned that when they are loved, protected, and properly cared for, your Inner Children live spontaneously and joyfully, with originality and energy—and they love you back.

In chapters 1 and 2, you read an overview of Inner Family Healing and learned how it relates to the Family Spell under which we all operate. You learned how to create a new, alternative vision to the Family Spell to lend direction and power to your healing process. Chapter 3 encouraged you to trust and validate yourself while going through the process. In chapters 4 and 5, you walked through the first and succeeding sessions, step by step.

Then, in the second half of the book starting in chapter 6, you read more about the underdeveloped Grownup and how to strengthen and educate it to care for the Inner Children. In chapter 7, Inner Sibling Rivalry, you saw a new way to look at addictions—as an interior power struggle between two or more Inner Children. In chapter 8 you read about the specific issues faced by Inner Children who've been sexually molested. Finally, in chapter 9, you learned about forgiveness, its myths, definitions, visions, and some processes leading to forgiveness.

We believe, based on the last 10 years of working with these ideas for ourselves and with clients, that the essence of healing is forgiving our many selves and thereby opening ourselves to the incredible richness that life can be.

Our prayer is that Inner Family work will take you a good piece along your journey. Ultimately, however, even after all your Inner Children have become peaceful and basically untroubled because of the care and protection that your Grownup provides, life will continue to present evidence that even more is called for in the way of reconciling you to life, the world, and the Spirit.

In that context, we encourage you to go beyond the Inner Family to explore and embrace your relationship with your Creator. As powerful as we've found Inner Family Healing to be, it is limited, for neither the Grownup, nor the Inner Children, nor even the whole Inner Family comprise the whole person. Therefore, wholeness means extending our embrace beyond the Inner Family to include the vastness of our wondrous subconscious, our souls, our spirits, probably our brothers and sisters in the world, the world itself, and only God knows what else.

So now that we have finally come to the last page, we wish for you the very best, and especially we hope that Mother Theresa's quotation is fulfilled by you and within you.

> ## "Every child has been created for greater things, to love and be loved."

May you have the best of a whole new life, and may the love of God bless you and everyone you meet along the way.

Shalom,

Jacqui & Mary

Appendix A

Joan: Case Example

Joan's marriage to Harry was deteriorating rapidly into shouting matches every night. The subject matter was always inconsequential, but the passions aroused were such that both of them felt their lives were at stake. One of them had only to make a mildly critical remark to start an argument, and by the time they had finished, not one relative or friend had escaped noisy, sarcastic censure. Joan began to see that one of her Inner Children was addicted to being angry and actually enjoyed being nasty. "But in the moment," she would say, "I'm so angry, I can't think straight. All I want to do is kill Harry off. Where's my Grownup then?" I'm like an alcoholic with this anger. How am I going to make a better life for myself?"

To stop the daily shouting matches, Joan needed to shut her mouth, breathe deeply, and take herself and all her Inner Children around the block for a walk so she could think straight. She couldn't do it; given the amount of rage she was feeling, Harry's goading, and the habit of years, Joan simply couldn't do it. "This Inner Child is too much for me. I couldn't control her if my life depended on it," she said. And she was speaking the truth. If someone yelled Fire!, Joan would no doubt have stopped and gotten out of the house. But it wouldn't be because her Grownup had the strength; it would be because her Inner Children also decided to pay attention to the threat of fire. Without the cooperation of the Inner Children, her Grownup wasn't strong enough to effect a significant change.

Parents handle willful children best when they are rested, calm, free from distracting influences, and unrattled by anger generally. The same goes for our Inner Grownups in relation to our Inner Children. No one handles things well when they're overtired. What Joan needed first was a break—

away from her responsibilities at home, away from work—time away from the cues that triggered this Child's addictive behavior.

So what Joan did was to house-sit for a friend for a few days. She told Harry she wanted to work some things out so she wasn't fighting all the time. And she left. The first thing she did on arriving at the house was to arrange for a massage. Here's the story in her own words:

> After the massage, I felt exhausted—not a shred of energy, but most important, not a bit of tension. For the next 48 hours, I only slept, ate, read, slept, and slept again. I didn't think about home at all, and I blocked out entirely the problem between Harry and me. I had asked the masseuse to return in a couple of days, which she did. After the second massage, I didn't feel so starved for human touch, and then I could begin to think.
>
> Throughout this time, I constantly gave myself encouragement and unconditional love: I'd say things to Joan the Grownup like, "You're a beautiful human being. You've done a smart thing by taking care of yourself. I'm glad you're alive. Look at the beauty here, the flowers. God put it all here and gave you the time to let yourself be fed by it." I closed my eyes, simply let God to look at me with love, and allowed myself to receive. I played beautiful music and I swam and took walks by streams. I looked at the sunset for an hour without pondering anything—I just let my thoughts run. I also told my Inner Children how much I loved them and wanted them to feel safe and happy. I told them how sorry I was that I'd been such an ignorant Grownup, and I asked them to forgive me. There wasn't much of a response, but at least I'd asked. They were still really angry—at me, Harry, and everyone else.
>
> The next thing I did was to write a letter to Harry that I had no intention of sending. I let it all hang out—the reasonable and the unreasonable, the love and the fear, hatred, and frustrations. When I reread the letter a bit later, I could see the different Inner Children responding. I could also feel Little One, who would love Harry no matter what he did. She didn't write, but I could feel that she wanted me not to care what he did, just love him. The other children were angry at her for not caring if he hurt them. I told them that Little One's ability to love Harry was important to us all, because she was also the one who could love each one of us that way, too.
>
> Then I asked myself, the Grownup, some questions and wrote down the answers.

1. Do I really love Harry?
2. What kind of commitment will I have to make to myself in order to keep sane and healthy?
3. What will I do or not do in the relationship?

I concluded that, because we are married, I would keep my part of the marital commitment, our vows, even though that might be the most difficult path for me and my Inner Children. To be successful, I would absolutely have to do several things:

1. Stay rested and get massage at least once a week to make sure I didn't get physically needy
2. Go cold turkey on my anger—give it up just like a nicotine fiend has to absolutely quit cigarettes or an alcoholic has to absolutely give up booze
3. Instead of nursing and indulging myself in anger, do the things on this list:
   — Shut my mouth
   — Breathe deeply
   — Take a shower or a long walk
   — Change the subject
   — Tell Harry that I would not allow myself to be provoked into being a persecutor
   — Sing the name of God
   — Give thanks for everything I can think of
   — Never let one Inner Child abuse another! For example, when I heard myself saying I was stupid, crazy, lazy, bad, irresponsible, or selfish, that was clearly a Child imitating a long-ago adult in my life, and I would say out loud, "Absolutely not. Do not pick on the other Children. I love you, and you don't need to do that. What is it that you really need?" Whether I got an answer or not, I would hug myself and change the subject. Later, when I was quiet, I would look for what was really going on with me, not Harry.
4. Nurture my Inner Children. Reassure them I would not abuse them or let anyone else do so. Tell them how beautiful, courageous, tender, and intelligent I thought they were. And they are. My Inner Children are a delight in my life.
5. Read this plan of action aloud at least three times a day. Also

carry it with me and tack it up on mirrors (I look in the mirror a lot).

6. Talk to people about what I was doing and ask for their support.

All these things reinforced my determination to be master of my anger rather than vice versa. Three items on the list were especially helpful:

- *Giving thanks.* I gave thanks for the air, my three meals a day, my hot showers, the fact that my body worked well enough for me to pee—imagine there are people who can't!

- *Making sure that none of my Inner Children abused the others.* When I caught one Inner Child abusing the others (like telling myself how stupid I was or naive to let Harry do such-and-such), I would ask forgiveness of all of them and then change the subject again.

- *Nurturing my Inner Children.* Writing letters to them was one of the best ways of nurturing. I'd buy beautiful cards and write little rhymes to my Inner Children. I'd put stickers on them, draw funny pictures, and put lovely bookmarks in them. I say things like, "I'm so lucky to have found you again." "If I'd had a daughter, I'd want her to be just like you." "Your love for me is what keeps me going some days." "Thank you for your willingness to trust me, even though I'm not a perfect parent."

I wouldn't have had to do this if I weren't a rage junkie, but I was. I used rage to "blow it all out"—to overpower all other feelings completely. Using something to blot out everything else is just like substance abuse. I used rage just the way a drunk uses alcohol. After I saw this, I took a cue from AA and admitted to myself and someone else every day that I was addicted to rageful feelings.

Someone who was afraid of his or her anger or handled anger in another way wouldn't have to do what I did. In fact, they should probably do the opposite. But for those whose temper tantrums are ruining their lives, this is a lifesaver."

There were days of despair when I wanted to give up, yet the declaration that I wouldn't helped me hang in. It wasn't easy, but gradually the Grownup began to win. By that I mean that I was able to see and hear my anger and stop it sooner. This took many months. I had a friend who was a social worker with clinical training, and occasionally she would do a session with me to help me get over a particular hump. I think therapy would have made it easier, but I wasn't willing at the time. I was still into all that silly stuff about having to do it myself. The fact is, I didn't do it all by myself anyway. Regular therapy just would have made it a shorter process.

Joan achieved a tremendous victory. It's helpful to analyze her story to see that what she did that enabled her to access the power to control her Inner Child's behavior.

1. She refused to continue engaging in a direct battle with her Inner Child.

2. She interrupted the Inner Child's addictive pattern by withdrawing from the triggering stimuli, no matter how much her Child wanted to stay in the fight.

3. She strengthened her Grownup by taking time out for her Grownup to rest, recover, be nurtured, and gather strength.

4. She obtained important information. Once rested and with the help of a loving but uninvolved friend, she examined the ways in which her Grownup allowed Harry to provoke her Child, and she worked out a strategy for dealing with triggering stimuli in a way that diverted energy rather than trying to block it.

5. She then responded directly to the tantruming Inner Child's underlying need for love and safety. She spoke with the Child, wrote dialogues and letters to the Child, played with the Child, and made sure the Child had enough rest and physical nourishment.

Joan's victory is especially impressive to those of us who feel helpless to change. It shows that even when one has an Inner Child who is very willful and strongly addicted (to anger, in Joan's case), and even when one has little or no truly adult modeling in one's childhood, one can still reclaim the power to take charge of one's behavior.

Appendix B

Diana and the Youthlings

In June of 1989, my husband and I separated. He could no longer tolerate a relationship with an absentee alcoholic and decided to see if he couldn't find something better. After setting up residence in an adjoining state and accelerating my attempts to drink myself to death, I decided to call the "Depression Busters," Mary and Jacqui.

Jacqui said that I needed to get in touch with my Inner Children. Being willing to try anything to stop the pain, I said "sure." I have always believed in magic,* and I have always believed in Mary and Jacqui, so this was not a fantastic suggestion to me.

Leona

The first Inner Child who made her presence known was Leona, she was living below my right rib cage. Leona is between six and seven. She was sitting on a chair in a dejected and dishevelled state in the middle of a large dance practice hall. Leona is the repository of all my feelings of abandonment. When I was her age, my nanny left to get married. She (Leona) was feeling hopeless and helpless because my husband had left and because she believed that she had to take care of herself (and me, an alcoholic just like my mother had been) and she knew she wasn't equipped to do that.

I held her (she's very affectionate), apologized for neglecting her (she's

---

* Magic for me is faith in the serendipitous nature of life, the goodwill and sense of humor of my Creator, unicorns and dragons.

very forgiving), cleaned her up, and dressed her in a lavender ball gown which she chose from all the dress-up clothes I used to have. This nurturing communication process continued for about a month with weekly guidance from Jacqui. On August 15th, while Jacqui and I were doing therapy, Mary called and said that God wanted me to stop drinking. I've often thought that Mary had an above average communication system with God (tho' sometimes I think they're not using AT&T so that the message gets garbled). I haven't had a drink since. Leona has changed her hair style, her costume, and she spends a lot of time dancing. She's no longer worried about being abandoned since she knows I'll never leave her and that I'm capable and willing to take care of both of us.

Leona thought that she had to be willing to accept abuse and neglect in order to get her needs met. She now realizes that isn't true.

Miriah

The next child who made her presence known is Miriah. I met her about 2 weeks after Leona. She is nine years old and is located under my right breast. Miriah first appeared as a carving on the front of an old sailing ship. She was in a very turbulent and stormy sea. She was wooden (numb) so that she wouldn't have to experience the fear of not making it to shore or the despair of never being able to stay in one place (port) for any length of time.

When I was nine, my mother sold our home and we moved to another state. That move precipitated a decision that nothing would ever last for more than 9 years. Both of my marriages ended after 9 years. I've lived in 21 different places since I was 9. My job requires that I drive 30,000 miles a year in four states to communities that change yearly.

This kid was tired and hopeless. Jacqui suggested that even though I might have to keep moving, there was no reason why Miriah couldn't have a permanent home. I discussed this with her and she thought it was a good idea. She could get off the boat and become flesh and blood.

With magic, we built her a house on a Pacific type of island within 500 feet of the ocean. The house is round, made of bamboo, roofed with thatch, and set on posts. When we first built it, it had 2 bunk beds.

Now that Miriah has permanence, I am able to plant perennials and trees, knowing that I may or may not be able to enjoy them for an extended period of time. This for me is a commitment to life, an acceptance of change (as opposed to a resentful resignation) and a real joy in creating something that will last.

I have had a real struggle this past year with my career (which has lasted 9 years this month). I discovered myself about a year and a half ago preparing to leave and sabotaging my chances of staying. This was a few months after I got in touch with Miriah. There are more Inner Children involved with this issue and I will discuss their involvement later. At least now I know I can choose whether to stay or not.

Dinan

Dinan is three. She now lives with Miriah, but when I first became aware of her she lived between my legs. She was a very provocative and sexual child who was making some crucial life decisions for me that were very inappropriate.

I have no specific memory of being sexually abused, but I do remember dreams of my mother and my aunt fighting over me that were of a sexual nature.

I don't enjoy pleasure without pain and have never had a long-term relationship with a man who was not well endowed enough to hurt. After I became aware of my choosing my partners based on penis size, I moved Dinan, my child who lived below my waist, in with Miriah.

I'm not complete on this issue yet. Dinan is enjoying just being a 3-year-old and really doesn't want to discuss it. I know that my criteria for a mate have changed and that I relate to men differently now. For the time being, that will suffice.

Temperance

Temperance was a prebirth child. She experienced the pain and discord and physical abuse that my mother experienced while she was pregnant. Temperance lived in my womb. She was very afraid of loud voices, confrontation, and men. Jacqui suggested I give her to Christ to hold. I couldn't because she was in an unfinished state and was too vulnerable to be touched. We decided to try rebirthing. I gave birth to her and handed her over to Christ, who holds her when I don't (which is most of the time). At first I felt like Maizy and Horton,* but she needed a lot more attention and

---

* Maizy and Horton are Dr. Seuss characters out of *Horton the Elephant*. Maizy is the lazy bird who persuaded Horton to sit on her egg for her while she played.

healing than I could give her. She's a very happy baby and a smart baby and a beautiful baby. She's no longer terrorized by loud and offensive people and neither am I.

❖

The next two children, Diana and Eloise, are my most cynical, intelligent, and defensive children. Diana is 13 and she lives in my head. Eloise is 5 and she lives in my heart. These inner Children have really been running the show in the absence of my Grownup being in charge.

Eloise

Eloise made a decision at the age of 5 that no one was trustworthy. She withdrew into a world of her own populated by her dolls, doormen, elevator operators, and domestics. Everyone else was observed. She discovered that most people don't listen, aren't honest with themselves or others, and prefer discussions about the inconsequential. She learned that to speak the truth about what she observed and felt was very shocking to those people. She was considered precocious. She had (and still has) some serious intimacy issues.

When I first saw her she looked like Eloise from the book, *Eloise at the Plaza*, with a very blase and cynical facial expression, poor posture, and an uncared-for sloppiness. After much coaxing, I was able to convince her to move in with Miriah and the other children. There was just one problem. When we built the house it had 2 bunk beds. Miriah and Leona had bottom bunks and Dinan had a top bunk. There was no way Eloise was going to take a top bunk, so we added a private sleeping alcove for Eloise. She shares in the activities of the other children and is still learning how to be a child. She still needs more time alone than any of the others, but she's finding out that having a family can be fun too. She no longer appears to me as a book character but looks like I did at that age. She's quite beautiful and very lovable (in a less prickly sort of way).

Diana

Diana still lives in my head (Christ and Temperance live there too).

When I was thirteen I tried to commit suicide. It was a serious attempt. I cleaned out the medicine cabinet and I lay down to die. I had been vomiting blood all night when my mother came in and started yelling at me. I told her she wouldn't have to worry about whatever it was that was bothering her much longer.

After they pumped out my stomach, she asked if there was anything she could get me, and I said I just wanted my father. My parents had separated when I was one and I had seen him once or twice a year since then. We weren't close. She called and told him what had happened and that I was asking for him. His response was "She's your problem."

I made several decisions that year: I would never trust any man. I had to be independent and in control, and I couldn't ask for help.

Diana does trust Christ and in a rebirthing session, He gave her a vision of a land of milk and honey. She sits on a couch that is large enough to accommodate the whole family, and the other kids come to her space for family conferences.

She is most like my father: proud, hard, unforgiving, ambitious, competitive, and aloof. My father is dying now and we haven't spoken for 27 years. I know now that the pride that allows that type of brokenness is wasteful. It has certainly trashed a good portion of my life. There is no real healing without forgiveness.

Sweet Thing

For the past three years I have had a condition which was eventually diagnosed as Laryngital Dysphonia. Nobody knows what causes or cures it. Hypnosis has been successful in treating some cases (not mine). The manifestations are a loss of voice or impairment similar to laryngitis and an uneven tonal quality with a catching on certain words. A friend once described it as a "you sound like a frog in a bag." When having phone conversations with people for the first time, they usually ask "Do we have a bad connection?"

The symptoms are worse when I am in a stressful situation (minimal when I'm talking to Jacqui and Mary or any other specialist who has attempted to diagnose or cure the condition).

When Jacqui first attempted to determine if an Inner Child was causing the problem, what I visualized can best be describe as "a hound from hell," snarling and snapping (we prayed that one away). It took a while before a short creature with hair hanging from head to toe allowed herself to be seen. If you've ever seen the old TV series "The Adams Family" and you remember "Cousin It," you know what she looked like. She wasn't interested in communicating or being seen. I got the impression that every time she was scared or angry, she was reaching up and grabbing onto my vocal chords.

Anger was an emotion that I was not allowed to express as a child "Children should be seen and not heard." And scared was not safe either. Choking off my anger had finally created physical consequences.

This child finally let me see her. I reassured her that it was OK to be seen and heard. She's just two, so she's not very verbal. We cut off her hair. She wanted to wear it like I wear mine. She moved in with Miriah and the other kids. She took the top bunk.

❖

When I have to work on a Saturday and my kids are unhappy and actually creating a stink, I pack a picnic and send them to the beach. Just because I have to work doesn't mean that they do. Diana and Christ even go on these adventures occasionally.

I was an only child, but not any more.

Appendix C

Notes for Therapists
on Theory and Practice

If you've read *How to Love Yourself* . . . , then you know that it is aimed toward clients, not professionals. Accordingly, theory constitutes a relatively minor part of its content and a good deal of what theory there is lies embedded in the explanation of the process itself.

This section, by contrast, aims at helping professional readers: (1) distinguish the theoretical constructs we're using from others, particularly those in transactional analysis, that one might assume to be applicable but aren't; and (2) lists the principal principles of practice we recommend adhering to in using this modality.

Theory

In gestalt terms, Inner Family Healing (IFH) is a way of dealing with figure and ground. The Inner Children's unmet needs are figures that persist and interfere with a person's ability to be in the present. When the Grownup establishes a pattern of meeting those needs, the figure recedes, and the person can be more present to current needs.

Transactional Analysis differs from Inner Family Healing in ways that concern the following constructs: (1) the Inner Children and TA's Child Ego States; (2) the Inner Grownup and TA's Parent and Adult Ego States; (3) the Critical or Pig Parent, which we consider to be an Inner Child; and (4) Games, which TA describes as external transaction sequences,.and which we see as both internal and external.

The IFH Inner Child Compared With TA's Child Ego States

The Inner Children differ significantly from the Child Ego State. Inner Family Healing treats the Inner Children as complete characters in themselves, both functionally and structurally. By contrast, the TA model ignores age both functionally and structurally, and instead breaks the Child Ego State down by behavioral criteria:

- TA's functional model divides the Child Ego State into Compliant, Rebellious, and Free.
- TA's structural model breaks the Child Ego State down into three parts the Parent in the Child, the Adult in the Child, also known as the Little Professor, and the Child in the Child.
- Both structurally and functionally, IFH divides child functioning into the individual Inner Children of different ages, each of whom manifest all emotions and attitudes—rebellious and stubborn, obedient, happy, sad, spontaneous—just like regular children.

How TA's Parent and Adult Ego States Compare With the IFH Grownup and Co-therapist

Structurally, the Grownup is not the same as the TA Adult or Parent. One way of describing the difference is to say the IFH Grownup combines the Adult operating in both analytic and intuitive modes with the best of the positive Parent ego state—that is, the positive or constructive Critical Parent and the constructive Nurturing Parent.

The Co-therapist, who we often call forth when a client is having trouble accessing the Grownup, looks a little more like TA's Adult Ego State because its main function is to perceive dispassionately. However, there are still two major differences between the Co-therapist and the Adult:

1. *The Co-therapist isn't responsible for making any decisions about caretaking of the Inner Children,* only for learning, seeing clearly, and coaching the Grownup.

   By contrast, the TA model's Adult is the person's primary decision maker.

   In the Inner Family Healing process, when Inner Children

are locked in combat, it's very hard for a Grownup to think straight, and the Co-therapist is like a consultant or adviser, a helper to educate and support the Grownup in carrying out its responsibilities until the Grownup has learned enough to do so independently. When the Grownup has learned enough to function independently, the Co-therapist tends to recede into the background, to re-emerge only when needed.

Accordingly, we teach the Co-therapist what we're doing in the moment—just as if the person were apprenticing with us. That way, we reserve no special knowledge to ourselves. If we dropped dead, the client would have as much familiarity with what was happening as we had time to impart, and they would also know that the power to change was truly theirs.

2. The Co-therapist incorporates the intuitive capabilities as part of fully matured thinking; we do not separate analytic from nonlinear perception and problem-solving. In TA, intuition is assigned to "the Little Professor," which resides in the Child ego state.

We prefer the Grownup over the TA model because it clearly assigns responsibility to one part of the person: The Grownup is responsible for the Inner Children, no matter what. The Co-therapist may be a useful source of information, but responsibility is vested in the Grownup and the Grownup alone.

The Pig Parent and the Inner Children

In TA, the Parent Ego State includes at least four components: the positive and negative nurturing parent, and the positive and negative critical parent. In practice, these ego states are revealed to be the introjected caretakers of the person's past, living in the personality like ghosts who continually moan the damning messages that created the problems to begin with.

The Inner Family Healing process doesn't recognize the existence of the original parents as parts of the personality, because doing so invites a person to continue seeing themselves as victims of their parents and makes it difficult for the person to accept full responsibility for their state of affairs in the present.

Instead, we have found the introjected parent to be an Inner Child who decided that the only way to be powerful was to be like the original parent.

That Inner Child may behave like the parent—usually does—and typically believes itself to be mature, but it's a masquerade. When a person's Inner Grownup gets educated and strong enough to reclaim the driver's seat from the masquerader "parent", the true age of this personality becomes obvious.

Games, Internal and External

Transactional analysis describes Games as external transaction sequences occurring between two human beings. In addition to that theory, we understand outer Games as manifestations of internal Games occurring among the Inner Children. (The section entitled Teach the Grownup to Identify and Interrupt Harmful Games in Chapter 6 sketches Game identification and treatment.)

What our strategy for dealing with Games amounts to is helping the client's Grownup: (1) take each of the warring Inner Children by the scruff of the neck, (2) hug them until they can think straight, (3) find out what they really need (which the Game playing is only a substitute for), and (4) meet that need on an ongoing basis.

Practice Suggestions

There's no way to fold into a few paragraph all the things we think and do in this work, and anyway, many of them are standard operating procedure for any good therapist. But here are some of the things that keep coming up over and over:

1. *Do the process yourself first.* If you haven't done this process, you can't lead someone else through it.
2. *Discourage transference.*
    a. *Do co-therapy, not therapy.* Invite the client to own the room as co-therapist with expertise in Inner Process, responsibility for getting information when it's missing for them, responsibility for getting a glass of water, being comfortable, etc.
    b. *Show your clay feet.* Share your own story where relevant, and your current struggles and failures. The client needs to know you've moved through your own battles and trage-

dies as a human being, not as an Extraordinary Special Person.

c. Trust the client, the Inner Children, and the process.

3. *Affirm that all Inner Children's needs, thoughts, and feelings are OK, no matter what*, and that the Grownup is the one responsible for actions.

4. *Affirm that the most bizarre behavior has a positive intent*, and that the aim of therapy is to update the information that prompted the original decision.

5. *Help the client to slow down thinking enough for the Grownup to hear things* from the Inner Children that it doesn't already know. If answers come too quickly, ask "Did that come from the Grownup or the Inner Child?" and be sure the client gives enough attention to hearing what they don't already know. If they consistently don't, then say something like, "I know you know it, I want the Child to hear it." Also, bring the client's Co-therapist in on the process of distinguishing Child voices.

6. *Clarify who's responsible for what and when.* For example, help the Grownup and the Inner Children see that the inappropriate responsibility the Inner Children took for their caretakers and other family members should not have been necessary to take. Also it may have been a fantasy devised to protect them from the pain of feeling helpless. If an Inner Kid took over and did something that created problems, it was still the Grownup's responsibility, not the Kid's.

One other thing, and that is, our first session is normally two hours, and many clients come for 1-1/2 to 2-hour sessions only about every two to three weeks. We may recommend a particular frequency of visits, but we leave the decision entirely up to the client's Grownup. We assert that our primary purpose is not to create long-term clients for supportive therapy, but to empower our clients to do their own therapy. If they want to accelerate the process, then by all means come, but it's not a prerequisite of either healing or working with us.

Bibliography

For Further Reading

Addiction

Black, Claudia, *It Will Never Happen to Me*. Denver, CO: M.A.C., 1982.
A little book which gives an excellent summary of dysfunctional family functioning; particularly good on family roles that people assume.

*Bradshaw, John, *Bradshaw on the Family*. Deerfield Beach, FL: Health Communications, 1988.
We recommend the tapes especially. Bradshaw's delivery and charisma make the complexity of his thinking entirely digestible.

Maxwell, Ruth, *Beyond the Booze Battle*. New York: Ballantine Books, 1988.
How to handle the challenge of family alcoholism. Excellent, concise.

*May, Gerald G., M.D., *Addiction and Grace*. San Francisco: Harper & Row, 1988.
This illuminating book examines addictions from a mental, behavioral, emotional, and spiritual standpoint.

Schaef, Ann Wilson-, *Codependency: Misunderstood, Mistreated*. New York: Harper & Row, 1986.
One of the best analyses of compulsive caretaking; identifies it, along with some 80 percent of other dysfunctional mental diseases, as a symptom of underlying addictive process.

Schaef, Ann Wilson-, *When Society Is an Addict*. New York: Harper & Row, 1987.
Ann Wilson-Schaef is one of the most brilliant theorists on the scene

---

* All bibliography items marked with * have been quoted in the text.

when it comes to addiction, codependency, and social manifestations of each. Not to be missed.

*Shainness, Natalie, *Sweet Suffering: Woman as Victim*. Indianapolis: Bobbs-Merrill, 1984.
CHAPTER 4 is HIGHLY RECOMMENDED for people who want to stop favoring the victim position.

Somers, Suzanne, *Keeping Secrets*. New York: Warner, 1988.
A powerfully articulated story of Suzanne's growing up in an alcoholic family and working through the addictive processes she adopted as a result. Provides hope for anyone caught in the trap of addition.

Woititz, Janet G., Ed.D., *Adult Children of Alcoholics*. Deerfield Beach, FL: Health Communications, 1982.
Another little book on the alcoholic family system, this one has sold over a million copies. Janet Woititz is one of the wisest and most compassionate voices in the field.

Emotions

Birnbaum, Jack, M.D., *Cry Anger: A Cure for Depression*. Don Mills, Ontario: General Publishing Company, Ltd., 1973.
An excellent description of how anger works. Especially useful is the boiler metaphor, which explains periodic blowups.

*Casriel, Daniel, M.D., *A Scream Away From Happiness*. New York: Grosset & Dunlap, 1972.
Available from the Casriel Institute in New York City. Casriel developed the New Identity Process, which combines touch and screaming for the discharge or integration of strong feelings. Although his orientation precedes Inner Family theory, this book is very good for people who need to learn about feelings, their logic, their expression, their nature, and one way to deal with old feelings.

Evans, Mandy, *Emotional Options: How to Use the Option Method*. Encinitas, CA: Option Learning Experiences , 1989.
Mandy also has an excellent tape. The Option Process is a gentle questioning sequence that exposes the magical thinking connected with the use of some feelings, and offers ways out of it. Write to: 1133-A Second Street; Encinitas, CA 92024.

Ford, Dr. Clyde W., *Where Healing Waters Meet: Touching Mind and Emotion Through the Body*. Barrytown, NY: Station Hill Press, 1989.

A finely researched and beautifully written account of discovery along the healing interface between touch and talk. Practical and scientifically sound. Ideal for the person leery of the touchy-feely world of alternative therapies.

Haldane, Sean, *Emotional First Aid: A Crisis Handbook*. Barrytown, NY: Station Hill Press, 1988.
Exactly what the title suggests: emergency treatment of emotional reactions to cope with crisis until more long-term solutions are available.

Hazleton, Lesley, *The Right to Feel Bad: Coming to Terms with Normal Depression*. New York: Doubleday, 1984.
Full of permissions for the Inner Children to feel what they feel, without judgment.

Zimbardo, Philip, *Shyness: What It Is, What To Do About It*. New York: The Berkeley Publishing Group, 1977.
Beautifully written, this book is recognized as a classic in the field. It addresses a subject affecting all of us, for shyness may be responsible for more failures and missed opportunities than any other single human characteristic. Shyness afflicts almost everybody on occasion, and a majority of us more or less chronically.

Games and Communication

As of this writing, we're still awaiting the definitive, readable book on Games. Berne's *Games People Play* was never meant for a lay audience. Someone, please! In the meantime, for the most up-to-date information on Games, call the International Transactional Analysis Association in San Francisco.

Bach, Dr. George R., & Ronald M. Deutsch *Stop! You're Driving Me Crazy*. New York: Berkley Books, 1981.
If you repeatedly find yourself getting into wild arguments that seem to make no sense and wondering about your sanity, this book is for you.

Berne, Eric, M.D., *Games People Play*. New York: Grove Press, 1964.
Written originally for a professional audience, this is not the most readable book, but it is the first, and so far, the only book we know of that provides an inventory of games.

Luthman, Shirley, *Collection*. Tiburon, CA: Mehitabel & Company, 1982.
A fine little book to help you stay with your own truth as you interact with others.

Powell, John, S.J. & Laura Brady, M.S.W., *Will the Real Me Please Stand Up? (So we can all get to know you)*. Allen TX: Argus, 1985.
Twenty-five guidelines for good communication: Excellent primer for expressing love, as are all of Powell's books.

Steiner, Claude, *Games Alcoholics Play*. New York: Ballantine Books, 1971.
This little book theorized that alcoholism was no more than a Game, a theory that Steiner later backed off from. However, it contains useful information about the Games that are involved in alcoholism, and is useful for anyone dealing with alcohol addiction.

Rebirthing

Nothing substitutes for actually doing a rebirthing series, and the lack of books that really satisfy testifies to that reality. So we recommend looking up rebirthing in your phone book and getting it first hand. However, those who prefer to get some advance information on it can try these two books.

Ray, Sondra, *Celebration of Breath*. New Orleans: Celestial Arts, 1983.

Sky, Michael, *Breathing: Expanding Your Power and Energy*. Santa Fe: Bear & Co., 1990.

Sexual Abuse

Chase, Truddi, *When Rabbit Howls*. New York: E.P. Dutton, 1987.
If Truddi Chase could do it, so can each of us. Not for the faint-hearted, this book is written by a woman who developed multiple personality disorder syndrome in order to cope with the most appalling sexual abuse. It is worth reading for several reasons: (1) it powerfully testifies that sexual abuse is never harmless; (2) it shows how the Inner Children, under the most extreme duress, rise to the challenge of survival as best they can; and (3) it shows how one woman, by determining to trust herself and by asking for help, navigated her way to freedom and power out of the most extraordinary horror by accepting and enlisting the aid of her Inner Children.

*Crewdson, John, *By Silence Betrayed: Sexual Abuse of Children in America*. New York: Little, Brown & Company, 1988.
Excellent overview of sexual abuse, particularly as it has been handled by the courts.

*Olio, Karen A., *Retrieval and Utilization of Memories in the Treatment of Adult Survivors of Sexual Abuse*. Unpublished paper, 1988.
Very good source of information on treating survivors.

Woititz, Janet G., *Healing Your Sexual Self*. Deerfield Beach, FL: Health Communications, 1989.
Simple, clear, wise.

Spirituality

Ensley, Eddie, *Prayer That Heals Our Emotions*. Columbus, GA: Contemplative Books, 1986.
Available from the publisher at Box 8065, Columbus GA, 31908.

Girzone Fr. Joseph F., *Joshua, Joshua and the Children*. Both New York: Macmillan, 1988, 1989
Two simply, wisely, and beautifully written books relating what the story of Jesus might have been if set in the 20th century instead of when it was.

Guideposts. Carmel, NY: Guideposts Associates.
A small monthly magazine for under $10.00 a year that is guaranteed to give you a lift.

Hunnard, Hannah, *Hind's Feet on High Places*. Wheaton, IL: Tyndale, 1979.
Inspiring.

John, The Gospel of John. New Testament.
Often referred to as the gospel of love. Pick a modern translation, such as J.B. Philips or the New English Bible version.

Lewis, C.S., *Chronicles of Narnia* and the Perelandra series. New York: Collier, 1970.
Allegories of the action of the Divine, of good and evil, of courage, and of love.

McNamara, James, *The Power of Compassion*. New York/Ramsey, NJ: Paulist Press, 1983.
An exploration of innocence and powerlessness as adversaries of the spiritual life, this book helps reconcile the apparent contradiction between "blessed are the meek" and loving oneself.

Pennington, Basil, *The Way Back Home*
No matter what one's religious or spiritual inclinations, centering prayer

is a very good way to begin opening up one's conscious experience of God, and this little book is a simple, clear introduction to it.

Philips, J.B., *Your God Is Too Small*. New York: Macmillan, 1987.
Explores the ways in which we limit our experience of the Divine, and how to get beyond them.

Powell, John, S.J., *He Touched Me*. Valencia, CA: Tabor Publications, 1974.
A moving autobiographical account of John Powell's own journey.

Sanford, Agnes, *Sealed Orders*. Plainfield, NJ: Bridge Publications, 1972.
An autobiography of a woman's journey out of chronic depression.

Steindle-Rast, Brother David, *Gratefulness, The Heart of Prayer: An Approach to Life in Fullness*. New York, New York/Ramsey, New Jersey, Paulist Press, 1984.
A classic not to be missed.

Thompson, Francis, *The Hound of Heaven*, available in a number of collections of poetry.
A profound and long-loved poem expressing the total commitment of God to winning our hearts and minds for loving communion with Himself.

Waters, Ethel, with Charles Samuels, *His Eye Is on the Sparrow*. Garden City, NY: Doubleday & Company, 1951.
This is a book that testifies to human courage—the will not only to survive, but to survive magnificently.

Other Important Books

*Fritz, Robert, *The Path of Least Resistance*. Boston: Stillpoint Publishing, 1986.
A definitive source of how-to's for creating new conditions in our lives.

John-Roger & Peter Williams, *You Can't Afford the Luxury of a Negative Thought*. Los Angeles, CA: Prelude Press, 1989.

Levinson, Harold N., M.D., *Smart But Feeling Dumb*. New York: Warner Books, 1984.
A wonderful explanation of dyslexia and learning discontinuities, what is coming to be called AAD—Ability Achievement Discrepancies. Such discrepancies afflict almost one-quarter of our population. For those of us raised before any understanding of AAD was generally available, this

can put an end to a lifetime of self-esteem difficulties that afflict our Inner Children.

Magid, Dr. James, *High Risk: Children Without a Conscience*. New York: Bantam, 1988.
In the interests of reversing some dangerous trends in this country, this brilliant, superbly written book examines some children's extremely destructive behavior patterns and how they originate. It is a priceless addition to any responsible lawmaker's desktop library.

Miller, Alice, *The Drama of the Gifted Child* (originally published as Prisoners of Childhood) New York: Basic, 1983.
A superb description and explanation of how we as children are impelled to surrender our own authenticity to care for our parents' wounded Inner Children, when they don't know how. Compassionate toward all generations.

Steiner, Claude, *When a Man Loves a Woman*. New York: Grove Press, 1986.
A book, by a man, for men, about relationships with women. One of those rare books that creates common ground between men and women.

Napier, Augustus Y., and Carl Whitaker, *The Family Crucible*. New York: Harper & Row, 1978.
An excellent presentation of family therapy, the need for it, the process involved.

Index